# CHASING WORTHINESS

## Advance Praise for *Chasing Worthiness*

"Tammy Sherger's book *Chasing Worthiness* is a must read! Tammy shares the ups and downs of her journey and in so doing provides superb insight, advice and guidance on how to lead a more fulfilling, courageous and successful life. She also reminds us that we are not alone in our day to day struggles and that we all have the capability to achieve our potential with the right mindset. Thank you, Tammy!"

**Nadia Bilchik**
CNN Editorial Producer
Author & Keynote Speaker

# CHASING WORTHINESS

The Journey from
Not Good Enough,
Smart Enough, Thin Enough,
or Any Other "Enough"

## Tammy Sherger

I AM
*Worth it*
PROJECT

NEW YORK

LONDON • NASHVILLE • MELBOURNE • VANCOUVER

# CHASING WORTHINESS
The Journey from Not Good Enough, Smart
Enough, Thin Enough, or Any Other "Enough"

© 2021 **Tammy Sherger**

Published in New York, New York, by Morgan James Publishing. Morgan James is a trademark of Morgan James, LLC. www.MorganJamesPublishing.com

ISBN 978-1-63195-054-4 paperback
ISBN 978-1-63195-055-1 eBook
Library of Congress Control Number: 2020902959

**Cover Design by:**
Kyla Werschke,
kylawerschke.com

Morgan James is a proud partner of Habitat for Humanity Peninsula and Greater Williamsburg. Partners in building since 2006.

Get involved today! Visit
www.MorganJamesBuilds.com

# TABLE OF CONTENTS

Preface     vii

**Section I: The Chase**     **1**
Chapter 1   Unleash Your Hidden Potential     3
Chapter 2   Stop Chasing And Stand Up     23

**Section II: The Choice**     **39**
Chapter 3   Speak Out     41
Chapter 4   I Love Money     55

**Section III: The Change**     **63**
Chapter 5   Living The Worthiness Lifestyle     65
Chapter 6   Execute It In The Real World     75
Chapter 7   The Success Connection     103
Chapter 8   The Unlikely Entrepreneur     109

About the Author     117

# PREFACE

Welcome! I am filled with gratitude for your willingness to share your valuable time with me. I am on a mission, a mission to help women stand up, speak out, and soar into the businesses, careers, and lives they are most passionate about. Because you—you, my love—are worth it and the world is ready for you to step into your passion. Can you feel it? Because I can. That is why I created the **I Am Worth It Project**.

After twenty-five-plus years of leading, coaching, and mentoring thousands of women, I have discovered the one missing ingredient. That ingredient is preventing you from living the life beyond what you ever dreamed possible for yourself—that life you only dare whisper to yourself. You don't want to share it with others because even you don't believe it is possible for you. That missing ingredient is your sense of worthiness.

If you can take the golden crown of worthiness and place it on your head every day, if you learn how to ensure that your worthiness tank is full, you will be changed. Worthiness will change the way you make decisions. It will change what you are able to do in the world. It will expand the options and reach not just for yourself but for others. We can, as fully worthy women, rise up and change the world for everyone—for every woman, every man, and every child. I am going to take you on a worthiness journey. Are you ready?

What's my promise to you? First, you are going to break through some limiting beliefs you probably don't even know you have right now. You are going to find your voice, and I'm going to show you how to use it. You are going to unlock the key to money and selling, because money and selling are not bad words. They are the fuel for your dreams. You are going to create the life you only dare whisper to yourself. You are going to be brave enough to do things that were once thought to be out of reach. You, my love, will discover how living the worthiness lifestyle is the secret path to the life you only now just wish for.

xoxo

Tammy

# Section I
# THE CHASE

# Chapter 1

# UNLEASH YOUR HIDDEN POTENTIAL

**W**e are going to unleash your hidden potential through the exploration of your right path. The challenge is that you may have adopted a path that seemed right but was not customized or designed for you. It was maybe right for your parents, a group of friends, or a college professor, but it was not uniquely yours. The path you have been on may have blocked your vision of living the life you only dream about. Your frustration with following that path may have blocked your view of your worthiness.

## The Right Path

Have you ever asked yourself that question, *Am I on the right path?* You know, *Are these decisions and directions right for me?* I have. I questioned where that right path comes from. I questioned where we get this idea of what the right path is. The path is from your family. It is from the culture you are brought up in. It's different for everybody. It's from your environment and the people around you. Sometimes where you live geographically will determine what you believe your right path is.

Here is what I believed my right path should be when I was growing up: I was supposed to graduate high school, otherwise I would never find a job. Honestly, the truth, when I was growing up, was more about getting a job than going to college. Get a good job, hopefully one with a pension, work there for forty years, retire, and have security. Along the way, get married, have two children, work hard, and buy a home. After that, buy a bigger home and a bigger car. Then raise those children, have some grandchildren, retire, and die.

If we stop to think about it, most of us do have this perceived right path we're supposed to follow. And if we don't follow it, we don't feel like we can be successful. Sometimes we're following it and asking, as I did at times, "Hey! Is this all there is? Shouldn't there be more?"

That's the question. I want you to think about that for a second. What do you believe is the right path? As you were growing up, what were you told was the right path to success and happiness? The messages you received about the right path and the people who told you are important when considering the impact on your life as an adult. They could have been people you looked up to. Together the message and the speakers set you up to follow paths that were right for them, but not necessarily right for you.

## Your First Job

I'm going to take you back to where I can recall being impacted by the "right path." I'm going to go back to my first job at Ponderosa Steak House. Can you remember your first job?

I was thirteen. I lied about my age to get this job. A dollar thirty-five an hour. Can you imagine that as your starting wage? I had to wear a nice little shirt and a cowboy hat. I was a bus girl. I cleared tables and sang "Happy Birthday" to children. I really, really needed that job because I wanted something: I wanted a pair of star jeans with the star on the back pocket. Oh my, they were designer jeans back in my day! And they cost twenty-five dollars. Although my dad worked hard every day, he couldn't afford twenty-five dollars for a pair of jeans. Hence, I was willing to put on that cowboy hat. Even if I didn't look cool while at the job, I was going to look cool when I went to school in my star jeans.

I learned belief number one while in this environment. It came directly from my parents, Toivo and Florence. My dad would say, "Just go to work. Go to work and work hard. Because if you work hard and you're good to your boss, everything is going to be okay." That's what I learned: to work hard. I took this belief to heart, and I developed a very strong work ethic. Much later in life I learned that working hard and waiting for people to notice was not going to guarantee success.

I jumped off my proposed right path. I dropped out of school, I was a teenage mother, and I was married before I was old enough to vote. If you look at the list of everything I was supposed to do to be on the right path, I wasn't.

Another belief was formed from these experiences. Success is for other people. Because I didn't take my parents' right path, I was never going to be successful. And there was nothing I could do to change that. I gave myself a life sentence. So, I didn't dream very big. And the beliefs snowballed from there. I'm not smart enough because I didn't finish school. I will never be successful because I was a teenage mother.

But is that really true? No. Think about what you believe to be the right path. What was the right path you thought you had to take? What beliefs did you develop from childhood? What beliefs are you carrying still? I carried my beliefs from childhood just like you. But I challenged those beliefs to become a different person, to define my own path. I found my worthiness.

What is worthiness made of? Worthiness is made up of your beliefs. And what is a belief? It's an acceptance, by you, of a statement. You decide that statement is true. That's the

*My dad Toivo in 1945*

*My parents, Toivo and Florence, 1950*

only thing a belief is. It doesn't matter what belief you have. It only exists and persists because you decide it to be true. Your decisions on what is true about yourself impact the way you are living your life.

All the words you tell yourself are made up in the context of the messages, the people, and your experiences. Things like I'm not good at reading. I've failed already. I'm not smart enough. Success is not for me. Worthiness—or its negative flipside, the feeling of unworthiness— is made up of all the beliefs you have. So I ask you to consider how important it is to be aware of the process that creates these beliefs. We are not aware of the origins and impact of most of our beliefs. Remember this: whether you believe you're worth it or not, beliefs are not true unless you decide they are.

## The Virtue of Judgment

Is it possible that judgment is good for you? Have you ever tried to stop judging other people? You might say, "I don't want to be a judger," pulling all the books and articles you can on the topic so you can discover the secret to stop judging. "I am such a bad person because I judge." But that's not true and here's why. You can't stop judging. I don't care what you read or what you do, you cannot stop judging because judging is natural to your brain network. Your brain is looking at what's happening around you. It's deciding whether those happenings match your beliefs. If they don't match, the judging rises to the surface. Those beliefs are strong and engrained. Your brain does not easily give them up, and it always uses beliefs to judge.

Let me give you an example. I love these belief-one-liners that really stick with us, like "children should be seen and not heard." When I was young, I heard that one a lot. Imagine you go into a restaurant and see this family, parents and their two children. The kids are having fun. They're coloring and being rambunctious. Sure, they're making a little noise, but they're not being bad. You sit down and think to yourself, *For goodness' sakes, can't that mother handle her children?* Notice you probably said mother and not father, so there's another belief. But are those children really being bad? Or is it because what's happening outside of you does not match what you believe? We can all recognize the feeling of judging, whether we are judging others or judging ourselves.

If I took you aside and asked, "What do you believe in?" you would likely respond, "I don't know," or list common beliefs regarding religion or politics. Most people have never examined the hidden beliefs that are driving their behavior. But if you use judging as a tool, you can immediately recognize where your beliefs lie. Whenever you get annoyed, uncomfortable, or upset when looking at someone else, these are the moments when you identify your beliefs. More importantly, when you're looking inside and hear that inside voice—your inner critic, as it is commonly called—you are also uncovering your beliefs about yourself.

Those are the prime opportunities to stop for a minute and ask, "Why is that judgment coming up? What is happening that does not match the way I believe it should be?" Always follow up by asking yourself, "Do I still believe this?" and "Does this belief still serve me?" The magic of this is that you can decide to

# Judgement is the barometer for your Beliefs 🖤

*Tammy Shenger*

@iamworthitproject

change your mind, delete the data, and get rid of beliefs that do not serve you in living your most passionate life.

## Defining Worthiness

Let's explore a worthiness definition. I employed Google, of course, to find a definition. Worthiness is the quality of being good enough. How much time have you spent chasing worthiness? Chasing the feeling of being good enough, smart enough, thin enough, or any of the hundreds of other types of enough we yearn for? Let me tell you, my love, no matter what you have done in your past, or what you will do in your future, just the way you are right now reading this page, you are enough. You, my love, are most definitely worth it!

## Empty Worthiness Tank?

I did not discover my worthiness until I was in my early fifties. Now you would not have known that from the outside. You would never have looked at me or what I had accomplished and said, "She doesn't believe in herself." I now recognize the

*My mom Florence, 1955*        *My mom Florence and my*
*grandma Lena Mador,*
*1955*

signs of an empty worthiness tank as they are so familiar to me. I carried them around for most of my life.

### 1. You are always working hard

You have developed a strong work ethic; you are usually the first one to start and the last one to finish. Without question you will notice tasks that need to be done and complete them without being asked. You are always willing to go the extra mile to finish a project or achieve a goal for others. Even though you have this strong work ethic, it seems as if no one takes notice of how hard you are working. Others around you appear to reap the rewards even though they are not working as hard as you. The problem here is that you remain in a constant holding pattern as you never ask for what you deserve but instead wait until it is given, and often it is never given.

### 2 Your emotions live at the surface

Every woman fears that moment of the dreaded tears when having a difficult conversation. I would say to myself, *Please don't cry, please don't cry*, as I headed into a meeting. At the highest level of my career, I was working around men almost exclusively. I was the only woman at the boardroom table, and all the executives around me were men. I'd go into a meeting knowing that I had to have a difficult conversation. I was always trying to figure out how to express it in ways that I felt would be acceptable to others. Then I would cry!

The men would look at me with puzzled faces. They didn't know what to do. Some would offer tissue and say, "It's okay, it's okay." But you could see on their faces that they were judging me in exactly the ways I feared. You could read the judgment on their faces: *She's too emotional. She can't control herself.*

But the reason why you are crying has nothing to do with being too emotional or not being able to control your emotions. The problem is that you're not living within your full sense of worthiness. And when you do not feel fully worthy, you do not speak out for what you want or stand up for what you deserve. When you continue to hold this below the surface, your emotions bubble up and run over, not because of what is happening in the moment but from not standing up for yourself over a long period of time.

### 3. You feel resentful

That feeling of resentment you keep hidden stems from always giving to others but not receiving in return.

The last lesson my mom taught me before she died at ninety-two was about the negative impact of holding resentment. My mom lived her life for her husband and children, and I never heard her complain about that. It wasn't until I visited her in the nursing home a few days before she passed away that she shared this truth with me.

I came for a visit, and perhaps because she had a bit of dementia (I think this is why because not once had she ever said this to me before) my mom said, "Tammy, I need you to promise me this one thing. You must go out and live your life to the fullest. I gave all my life to my children, and I love you. I love all of you. But I didn't do anything for me. Tammy, you know I loved all my children, but now at this point, I regret not ever doing anything for myself. Don't do that. Go out, go now, and do everything that inspires you, because before you know it...

"One day, Tammy, if you live long enough, you will be standing in my shoes; your time will have run out and it will be too late. Time will go by fast, and if you don't go after your dreams, if you don't follow what makes you happy, you will resent it. And it will be too late to fix it."

My mom had many talents. Talents as a homemaker, as a mother, at anything I ever saw her attempt. She was also a talented writer. It was only when I was older and going through some of the family photo albums that I discovered Mom loved to write.

I found dozens of poems and short stories written on pieces of paper, probably written late at night when she had a moment to herself. And she was good!

She never pursued this passion, though. She never put herself first.

Mom would keep these poems she wrote tucked away on scraps of paper, writing late at night when she had moments to herself. I have several of these poems. After she passed away, I said, "You know what, Mom? We're going to make you an author." And in honor of my mother we created a book of her poems. If it's okay, I will share one with you right now that she wrote for me.

You have a lot of inspiration. And a lot of talent too. You're a credit to your family and we are proud of you. You had some fears and cried some tears, but you're determined to go on. I always will be here for you, to keep you calm and strong. You are a treasure, that's what you are. There is no doubt, you are a star. Love your mom.

One of my favorite memories of my mom is when she wrote her name. She would always say, "I have eight letters in my first name and eight letters in my last: Florence Pyykonen." Thank you for allowing me to honor my mom by sharing that poem with you. If you constantly give to others and get nothing in return, if you always put everyone else first, you will end up living in resentment.

Giving to yourself first, putting yourself first, is not selfish; it is a magical gift that you give to others. It sets an example for them to follow. It shows them the roadmap for a passion-filled life.

From a place of full worthiness, you can offer others the highest version of you! And what could be better than that? Nothing!

What are you putting off until tomorrow? Don't wait until it's too late and your time has run out.

## The Aha Moment

If you are feeling the signs of an empty worthiness tank and this narrative resonates with you, I need you to know something. You don't need to live that way. You deserve to live the life you are most passionate about.

I want to share with you how three little words changed my life. They came in response to a question I asked my doctor. I was thirty-six years old, diagnosed with stage two breast cancer.

"Am I going to die?" I asked. He spoke words that have become my reset button.

"I don't know," he said. I don't know. In that moment, in that doctor's office, I took those three little words as a revelation. I realized I had run out of hope. I had run out of time. I was filled with an overwhelming sense of regret. Regret for the things I hadn't said. That I hadn't done. But mostly for all the things I would never have a chance to become.

I must tell you; I can still feel being in that room, in that moment of despair. *Oh my God, how can it be over? What do you mean I'm going to die? I don't have any more time left?* I hadn't written all I wanted to write. I hadn't traveled or danced. I hadn't done any of the things I'd whispered quietly to myself. I hadn't done any of that because of my belief that I didn't follow the right path. That success was not for me. That I wasn't good enough. I was not worthy.

That was the day death became a close reality for me instead of a distant event that would take place far off in my future. None of us considers our mortality until we are faced with a life-threatening situation. However, you don't need to wait for that; you can learn from my lessons. I made a promise to myself that day that if I lived, I would never face that feeling of regret again.

That one moment took me on an extraordinary journey travelling from deep despair and overwhelming regret to being able to follow my true passion and live my life beyond what I had ever dreamed possible for myself as a young girl.

That moment of regret started a twenty-year journey for me. I've been twenty years cancer free now. My journey started with a commitment to myself, that day, to live without regret. What I didn't know was that it would also lead me to discover how worthiness was the missing ingredient to living my dreams.

No matter what I had to do, I was going to make sure that whenever my final moment came, I would know without a doubt that I had lived unapologetically and completely. I hoped that I had more time to redeem. I didn't know when the final moments would be. I was going to find out if I was going to live after a process of treatment and recovery. I still had a mountain of medical treatment to go through. If you are unaware of cancer treatment, there is an excruciatingly long period between a diagnosis and the moment when somebody says you have hope. Another biopsy remained before they would provide me with any information other than malignancy. That test returned. I had a lumpectomy and submitted myself to treatment.

It was after surgery that I finally heard there was hope. The cancer hadn't spread to my lymph nodes. That time between diagnosis and surgery gave me too much space to sit in regret. My promise wasn't just about staving off regret. It was about living each day to its fullest.

## Planting the Worthiness Seed

I want to share the poem I wrote shortly after that day in the doctor's office. Perhaps you or someone you know has experienced a cancer diagnosis and this poem illustrates the shock of facing your own mortality. I have since learned not to be afraid of death but to be aware that it exists. None of us can escape this part of the human life cycle.

### I Have Cancer

You have cancer. Can you check the name on the file please? You have cancer. Are you sure this diagnosis is for me? Am I going to die? You have cancer. I don't know whether to scream or cry. The thought whirls through my head. You have cancer. All the times I have chosen. Tomorrow. Instead. Too many times. A life lesson learned. I have cancer, the lesson I know is to not leave undone any hopes that I hold.

I didn't know it at the time but that was where the seeds of the I Am Worth It Project were planted. I thought I was making sure that I never lived with regret. What I didn't realize

# YOU ARE NOT ALONE 💙
## Somewhere there is
## Someone who feels
# JUST LIKE YOU 💙

*Tammy Sherger*

@iamworthitproject

at the time was that in order to do that I had to find my self-worth. And that is how I discovered the most powerful and under-utilized tool we all have that can impact our greatest transformation.

## Your Power Tool

The most powerful tool you already own is your brain. Your very own personal computer. The problem with the brain, when left to its own devices, is that it will continue to make decisions from decades-old data. When I am giving a talk, I always ask my audience if their brain is operating like a Commodore 64.

I attended a talk about artificial intelligence recently by one of Canada's top scientists. In this talk he mentioned three Canadian scientists who won a prestigious award for their work in advancing artificial intelligence. Well, do you want to know how they did that? They modeled the human brain. Simply put that's how they figured out how to put the right data into a computer to get the right answer out. As humans we fail to consider that the data we put into our brain in the form of thoughts—what we hear, see, and experience externally, and how we talk to ourselves internally—will drive our behaviors.

We are not taught to manage the flow of information to our brain, to become proactive instead of reactive and train our brain. Instead, for most of us, we are living what I call the robot life with our brain in charge and operating in a fully present mode only 5 percent of every day, according to scientists. Imagine what you could accomplish if you increased from 5 percent to 15 percent of the day being fully present in your life? What new ideas would jump out? What dreams could you realize?

I have discovered that our brain is the most underutilized tool we all have that can impact our greatest transformation.

Your brain has the ability to help you accomplish all that you dream of and deserve. But most of us just let our brain run wild on its own with no guidance or input.

Sounds dangerous when you hear that, doesn't it?

If we had to go through Brain Training 101 early in life, we could avoid some of the common pitfalls and roadblocks we all face on the road to success.

Your brain is your very own personal computer.

And your words—the ones you say out loud, the ones that come from your inner critic, and even the words you hear from others—are the DATA you are feeding into your personal computer.

On the other side, that data comes out in the form of your behavior. The data you feed into your personal computer drives your behavior

Is it time for you to review and delete data? Do you want a Commodore 64 running your life? Computers have been updated since the days of the Commodore. That 64 referred to the 8-bit architecture of the computer. Computers these days are 64-bit architecture. Even your phone is at least 32-bit. You must upgrade.

In the age of Netflix, we have welcomed a new term into our culture: binge watching. We can't stop watching because they leave us hooked at the end. I read an article that said Netflix has the goal to be able to know you through your recent viewing history. They use this data to choose what shows you see based on the shows you have already watched. Their ultimate goal is for you to be able to open your Netflix app and for them to be able to start playing the show they know you want to watch based on your previous viewing history. Think about that for a second. In the future, they want to be able to take your data based on past behavior and predict what you will want to watch in the future. There would be no room to evolve or make different choices. No room to grow or change your mind. You wouldn't even know what you are missing out on because you would never have the opportunity to see it for yourself and decide in that moment if you want to watch it. I don't want to be making the same choices today that I made twenty years ago. I want to be able to experience fully all that life has to offer, knowing that I will always continue to evolve and change.

What about the data that has been entered into your own personal computer, your brain?

Do you want your life to be run with twenty-year-old data? You no longer make conscious choices or try anything new. You will live the rest of your life watching the exact same shows because you're not going to be exposed to anything else. That's exactly what many of us are doing with our brains and our lives. You're not changing the data, the input. You are living the ROBOT LIFE.

My greatest teachers about the power of the brain have been my two grandchildren, Hunter and Annabelle. I made a promise to always be fully present with them. That is not possible as a parent when you have so many other responsibilities, but as a grandparent, I am able to meet this most of the time.

I have seen and scientists report that you are basically in a hypnotic state from the time you're born until you're about eight. We are, quite simply put, being programmed. You're taking in all this data, your beliefs, values, norms, and experiences. *I'm*

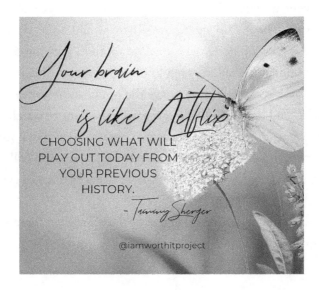

*Your brain is like Netflix*
CHOOSING WHAT WILL PLAY OUT TODAY FROM YOUR PREVIOUS HISTORY.

— Tammy Sherger

@iamworthitproject

*on the right path. No, I'm not. This is good. This is bad.* But as a child, your brain does not have the ability to decipher what information to keep or not. And guess what you do with all that data? You carry it into adulthood as your beliefs: "Here I am. This is who I am, world. I can't read, but I'm good at math. I don't like to speak in front of people because I'm very shy." You bring all of this to adulthood with little or no questioning. Most of us will live almost our whole lives believing stuff that is not true and is only data. Many of us are not upgrading and reprogramming our brains. The good news is that whatever has been programmed can be reprogrammed. That is why you must learn how to train your brain.

*My granddaughter Annabelle*     *My grandson Hunter*

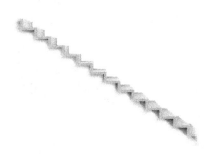

# Chapter 2

# STOP CHASING AND STAND UP

S tand up for yourself. Stand up for your own value. It sounds like a rallying cry for resistance, maybe even revolution. Most would think of standing against, but I am providing you with a different take on standing up. We must decide that we are not going to wait to be noticed, to have other people decide what we are worth. It is time to discover how to stand up for yourself. At any time, you can choose to write a new story for your life. We're going to talk about letting go of who you are now to become who you are destined to be.

## Rewrite Your Story

If you want something you've never had, whatever it is, you must be willing to do something you have never done before. I want you to think about that. If you want to be a speaker, if you want to get a new job, if you want to go back to school, you're going to have to do something you've never done before. And as soon as you step outside your comfort zone your brain will go into protection mode and you will face a steady stream of thoughts telling you NOT to do what just a minute ago seemed like a great idea.

I was six weeks into my cancer treatment, having had surgery. They tell you how tired you will feel with chemotherapy, but until you live through it, you just can't understand. So there I was sitting alone on my sofa, unable to even imagine the strength to get up, pick up the broom, and sweep my floor. I was only thirty-six years old.

I turned on the TV instead, and the *Oprah* show appeared. I can't tell you who her guest was, but I clearly recall Oprah talking to an audience member who was listing every bad thing that had happened to her.

The audience member said those bad experiences were why she could not live life to the fullest.

Then Oprah asked her a simple question—one I almost missed because I was so busy wallowing with the audience member. Agreeing with her.

Oprah asked, "Is it possible that you could change this story?"

I was busy thinking to myself, *Yes, I relate to you. I took the wrong path. I dropped out of school. I was a teenage mother, married before I was old enough to vote. I lived with domestic abuse for sixteen years, and then I got cancer.*

And it was all true. After all that who wouldn't feel sorry for me?

But Oprah's question sparked a small flash of insight. Suddenly I could see that I was the one keeping my life in perpetual crisis.

And at that moment I thought maybe I could change my story.

I got up off the couch and decided to take my regular walking route, one I used to walk before I was sick. *I am going to change my story,* I thought. Filled with inspiration from Oprah, I headed out. Having just made it halfway through my route, I tripped and fell. I hit the sidewalk with painful force, skinning both my knees. I stayed down there crying. Internally, I was shouting, *I should have stayed on the couch! I should have stayed in my other story because at least I would be safe now.*

There were no cell phones in that day. At least I didn't have one. I stayed there on the sidewalk for an extended period. "Okay," I said to myself. "You have to get up. Okay?" But I'm crying. You know that cry where the tears are staining your face? Snot dripping unattractively from your nose and no Kleenex in reach? Pulling myself up and crying my eyes out, I made my way back home.

I collapsed on the couch feeling sorry for myself and reached up to push the hair out of my face. My hand came back down filled with my long golden locks of hair. It was happening just as the doctors predicted. I was losing my golden crown of glory. This hair that had identified me since childhood. The hair that was the subject of stories my mother told of rags she used to create the ringlets that dripped around my face. Now it was in my hand.

I know other women can relate to their hair being tied to their identity. I reached back up, and yes, the hair was falling out of my head. I called my sister. "I'm pulling my hair out of my head." Usually that means you're having a crazy bad day. That's the meaning she understood.

"What's the matter?" she said. "Are you okay?"

"No," I blurted out, "I'm literally pulling my hair out." It is something I laugh about now, but not at the time.

I bet you have had this moment. You made a decision in a moment of inspiration that you're going to change. Has that ever happened to you? You get this inspiration to get up and make a change. As soon as you do, the very next thing that happens is BAD. You say to yourself, *Well, what's the point? Nothing will ever be any different.* I was inspired when I left for the walk until I fell.

I felt justified in feeling sorry for myself. After all, I had taken the wrong path, so success would be for other people. I had escaped from an abusive marriage, but to do so I had to leave behind all the wealth we had accumulated while we were together. Now I had cancer and my hair was falling out. Can you relate to my story?

Yet my commitment to erase regret was so fresh that this day I made a different choice than to wallow in my sorrows. I decided right there that it was time for me to cancel my pity party. Hell, I was grateful to be alive. Being alive meant that I had hope. I had a chance. That's hope for a brighter future. I made a choice that day, a choice to tell my story in a new way. I was going to rewrite this story of overwhelming regret and turn it into a full-blown bestseller of inspiration for myself and others.

You can, at any time, choose change. You can, at any time, rewrite the story. You really are the author. In that moment, I made a change. I affirmed a decision. Whatever you're telling yourself, it's a story. And I'm not saying it's not true, because believe me, we could all stand up and go story to story, couldn't we?

The big questions concern whether that story serves you. If it does not, it is time for a rewrite. In that doctor's office that day, I was diagnosed with stage two breast cancer. I learned the hard way. I can guarantee you this: one day your time will run out. And you want to be living the life you're most passionate about. I'm telling you from experience, you don't want to have that moment of overwhelming regret. You can let go of who you were and become who you want to be. A life lived well is always evolving.

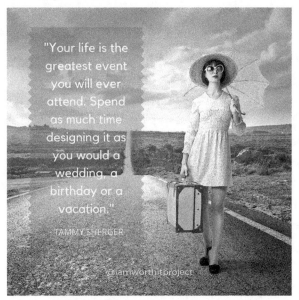

"Your life is the greatest event you will ever attend. Spend as much time designing it as you would a wedding, a birthday or a vacation."

TAMMY SHERGER

@iamworthitproject

## Stand Up and Sell

Why include selling in a book about worthiness?

Because you can't build a life, business, or career you are passionate about unless you can sell. Even if you are a not-for-profit, you must sell what you are doing to other people who will then give you money to support your cause! Women must stop waiting for someone else to notice their value, for someone else to ask for their service, product, or expertise, and someone else to decide their worth. It is time for women to STOP saying, "I just want to help people." *If I help people the money will follow* is a MYTH that prevents women from increasing their wealth and impact in the world. As women we can no longer continue to live inside these cultural fairy tales that most of the population has adopted as true.

## I Am Not a Salesperson

I hear this from women all the time. "No, I'm not selling because I don't like selling. I am not a salesperson."

Do you hate selling? Does the very mention of *cold call* have you running in the other direction?

Does the thought of asking for a sale give you that dreaded feeling in the pit of your stomach? And you keep saying to yourself, "I can't do this. I'm not a salesperson."

Well, you are not alone. Not too long ago I was just like you. I felt exactly the same way. If it's okay I would like to tell you a quick story of how I transformed my relationship with SELLING.

I had been successful in business for over twenty-five years and grew my career from a clerk to a senior executive driving multimillion-dollar initiatives and multiple teams, and along with a small group of people I built a startup company from zero and an idea to a $125 million market cap. I had reached the point where I had achieved more than I thought possible for myself as a young girl. I was at the top of my game and earning more money than I ever imagined I would in my lifetime. And then I decided to become an entrepreneur.

Now, in the various roles over my career, I had always been in operations. I was the operational strategist; if there was a problem, I would get sent in to fix it. I had never been in a sales role. I had overseen contract negotiations, sat at the boardroom table, but I had never been the person who had to make my living based on closing that sale.

I have to tell you; I underestimated the challenges of becoming an entrepreneur. Believe it or not, that selling thing never even crossed my mind as an obstacle.

At first when I was coming up with my idea, my branding, and my processes, everything was great because I was in my comfort zone, in operations. I was doing what I had always excelled at. I did tradeshows for market research, and that came easy to me because it was about talking to people and collecting business cards. But here's the thing: if I wanted to build my business, I was going to have to make use of those business cards. I was going to have to SELL.

Now this is a personal part of my story about my first cold calling adventure, and I want to share it so you can understand how deep the fear of sales ran in me.

I have a son, bless him, who is a natural-born salesperson and a natural-born entrepreneur. He could sell anything to anybody.

He also knew that I didn't like sales, and so he said, "Mom, you know what? Let's go out together the first time and do some cold calling." So I agreed.

The day of the cold calling arrived, and I had all my stuff together and was waiting for my son to get to my door—but I have to tell you I didn't want to go. I had this sinking feeling in my stomach. I had all these thoughts running through my head like, *Hey, I'm a senior executive; I can't go out cold calling. Are you kidding me? I don't want to do this. I don't want to sell. I am not a salesperson…*

However, on the other hand, I was still a parent and had my son coming to pick me up, and I couldn't say to him, "I'm not going. I am too afraid…"

My son arrives and off we go on our adventure.

At the time I lived in the downtown area of my city, so it was easy to access businesses and for me to make my three cold calls.

Now this was a true role reversal. Here was my son walking me to do a cold call when I had walked him many times to the first days of school.

And my son kept saying, "Don't worry about it. You are not there to sell anything. It's just practice." Well, I'm proud to say that I did complete those three cold calls, but that was also the day I decided there had to be a better way. I was never going to be like my son. I wasn't a natural-born salesperson, and this didn't come easy for me.

At first I spent hours on Google researching sales techniques, looking at all the leading salespeople to see what they were doing. Talk about information overload

Then I decided I was going to take some sales training—but that didn't help me because it didn't change the fact that I still hated sales.

I considered this statement that I hear all the time: "People do business with people they like." I thought, *Hey, I'm a likeable person, but that's not helping me close sales.*

Perhaps you are in the same spot I was in. I had burned the bridges, abandoned the lifeboats that would take me back to a "job." There was no going back. I couldn't let this fear, this distaste for selling, prevent me from achieving my dream of having a successful business.

And then finally I had that moment. You know what I mean—that aha moment when things become clear. For me to have my own business, I had to be able to sell. I also knew I had to figure out how to do this by using the operational skills I had always excelled at. The sales strategies and training that other people were teaching were not going to work for me.

I needed a system to wrap myself in, a system that would work and would also make sales comfortable for me. So that's what I did. I created my very own sales operating system, my own life preserver, so I could keep my dream of being an entrepreneur and building a business alive.

Building a successful business is not just about people liking you or being good at building relationships, because that leaves everything to chance.

What will make your business successful is a sales operating system that will keep your clients saying YES at every step of their journey with you and your business... When you have created an optimum CLIENT environment, a winning client experience that keeps your clients saying YES to you, your brand, and your business. You strategically plan it every step of the way; nothing is left to chance.

And, YES, it is still selling.

Here's the thing. We have been selling since the beginning of time. We sell our expertise, our products, our services. We sell ourselves at job interviews, when we are dating, and even Mother Nature is selling to us when we look out the window first thing in the morning to see if it is sunny, raining, or snowing.

As a culture we have designated selling as a bad word. We have made it difficult for hardworking small business owners and entrepreneurs to SELL their products or services without having that underlying fear, that angst in the pit of their stomach that they are doing something that is NOT socially acceptable!

So what do they do? They don't sell or promote their products or services, and their businesses and dreams suffer.

Bottom line: you can't own a business if you don't have sales. It doesn't matter what role you hold in a company, or whether you own the business or are an employee. It doesn't matter if we discuss business or your personal life; we are always SELLING.

But if you have a sales operating system, your very own SOS—a life preserver—where you can make selling feel comfortable, then you can have your dream as big as you want. You can live beyond what you believed possible. Sales isn't just about asking that one question, making that cold call. Sales is in every detail. It's about having a system that allows you to create an entire client experience, an entire client environment where everything you do is leading your client to keep saying YES over and over again. Sales don't happen by accident.

So if you are like me and the mere thought of sales has you running in the other direction, but you also know that if you don't make your sales happen your dream of having your own business and being your own boss will die, then let me be the person to throw you a life preserver.

I now teach my personal sales operating system to people around the globe who find themselves stuck in the FEAR of selling.

If my son had not pushed me out the door that day, I wouldn't have gone. And I would not be here right now. I never would have faced my fear of asking for a sale. I would have remained stuck in my negative beliefs about why selling is bad. When really it was not about selling at all; it was about my own worthiness. It was about not believing that what I was offering—my product, expertise, or service—was worth what I was asking for it in return.

## Selling Is an Exchange of Value

You offer your product, service, or expertise and your client gives you money.

You can LOVE what you do and HATE to SELL. But you can't sustain what you LOVE if you don't SELL

Tammy Sherger

@iamworthitprojectt

## The Selling Myths

**Myth #1** Selling is sleazy.

<u>Fact</u>—Do you believe that your potential clients will be better off after they have done business with you? That's why you are in business and how clients lives are transformed.

**Myth #2** If people want to purchase my product or service, they will ask me for it.

<u>Fact</u>—No, they are going to buy from someone else who will ask for the sale, who has been persistent and has demonstrated value.

**Myth #3** I am not a natural salesperson so I can't sell.

<u>Fact</u>—It is likely that you haven't had to sell before so what you are really feeling is fear. When you can acknowledge the

fear, you can open yourself up to using a system for selling that works with you not against you.

**Myth #4** People will get annoyed with me if I call, email, or stop by their business.

Fact—Just like you, most people are overwhelmed with the number of emails, phone calls, and tasks they have to accomplish each day. You are not top-of-mind for them. Your job is to stay connected, top-of-mind, by adding value in every interaction. Send a tip, checklist, or resource that will instantly help them. Be of service and you won't be an interruption or a bother.

**Myth #5** I love what I do and I'm good at it. Shouldn't that be enough to grow my business?

Fact—No! Being good at what you do is not enough. How will anyone know about you, your experience, or your expertise if you don't sell? There is a currency in the world that is constantly being exchanged, and it's called money. You are exchanging value (your expertise) for value (your client's money).

Here's the biggest myth of all. I bet you have heard this before: selling is about relationships. Business is about relationships. When people like you, they're going to buy from you. I'm not going to lie. I want people to like me, and I think I'm pretty likable. But I'm going to tell you, even if I get you to buy once because you like me, that's not going to sustain my business. Building a successful business is not just about people liking you or being good at building relationships, because that leaves everything to chance.

In order to receive money, every single person is selling their expertise, services, or products. However, almost without exception, every woman I meet gets that terrible feeling in the pit of her stomach when she must ask for a sale, a raise, a promotion, or anything.

SELLING has become a bad word. You know the kind of word you can't say in public without receiving disapproving looks. When I am out in public with my grandchildren and they overhear such words, they will say, "Grandma, that person just said a bad word. I can't say it, Grandma. But you know the one I mean. It starts with an F." Okay, we all know what the F-word is. We can't say that F-word, so we will replace it with words that are more socially acceptable like fudge, flippin', or my all-time favorite, frick.

Now I am not proposing that we all go out and start using the F-word or its more acceptable cousins. What I am suggesting is that we have other words in the English language that we have designated as bad words. Here's the thing. You, every day, are always SELLING.

It is entirely possible to have a hobby you love to do, and you just GIVE everything you create or build away for free. However, you still must SELL people on coming to take it for free.

But first we must SELL. Instead of saying that BAD WORD, selling, now women have come up with more socially acceptable words like relationship selling, heart-based selling, value selling, and the list continues.

By designating selling as a bad word, we have made it difficult for women to SELL their products, services, or expertise without having that underlying fear, that angst in the pit of their stomach that they are doing something that is not socially acceptable. So what do they do? They don't sell or promote their products or services, and their dreams and goals suffer.

Do you know what a client or customer really wants? They want you as a person to DELIVER the service, product, or transformation you PROMISED when you were SELLING! When you DELIVER then you are creating value and relationships. For any business to DELIVER they first must SELL. If you don't like the way someone is selling something, don't buy from them. If you don't want what someone is selling, just say no! SELLING is not a bad word! SELLING keeps our economy rolling. Failing to DELIVER what you SELL…now that is bad!

Worthiness and selling go hand-in-hand.

As I said, selling is an exchange of value. I really believe that. I know that if I stand in a training and believe in what I have to offer, you're going to know it. I also know this: if you don't want it, I'm okay with that because you can just say no. We all have the right to say no when we don't want something.

I notice this on Facebook quite often where various people will post their distaste for other people who have "friended" them and then immediately send them a selling message. What if you changed that around, and even if you don't want what they are offering, you sent that other woman a note congratulating her for being brave enough to ask for the sale? "Thanks so much for letting me know what you are doing. I really admire your bravery to go out and sell. I'm not interested right now." And what do you think that does for that other person? It allows her to put her energy into other opportunities. It allows her to feel proud and confident in building her business.

I have found that most people who dislike people who ask for the sale do so because they don't like to say no. It makes them feel uncomfortable.

If we are going to rise together and support each other as women to fill our worthiness tanks to overflowing, we need to increase our earning power. We must embrace selling.

When we as women increase our overall level of wealth, we widen our ability to impact the changes we want to see in the world.

## Section II
# THE CHOICE

Chapter 3

# SPEAK OUT

**Y**ou have forgotten how to speak out and ask for what you want, or maybe you have never known how. Are you holding tightly to a secret dream, a life you only whisper in your deepest thoughts? I know I was. I was waiting for someone to validate my worth before I could go after the life I was dreaming of.

There is a method to asking for what you want, speaking up for what you deserve. This is a skill you can develop. When you decide to speak out you are setting boundaries and expectations for who you are and how people can treat you.

## If You Don't Ask

We have all headed into a sales meeting, a discussion about a raise, or a difficult conversation. We have had that sick feeling in the pit of our stomach and maybe even an overwhelming cloud of dread. We know what we want, but we're not sure we have the courage to ask for it.

This one salary negotiation meeting was a turning point for me. The experience empowered me to ask for what I wanted. I had been with this startup company for just over four years when this personal meeting story took place. I had been preparing for my year-end meeting, setting the agenda of topics I was going to discuss with my boss regarding my performance and salary review. On the night before the meeting, I had a phone conversation with my son discussing what my strategy should be in the meeting. At the close of that conversation my son said to me, and I quote, "Mom, it's not that they do not value you, it's that you do not value yourself."

In that one moment this became the proverbial straw that broke the camel's back. That one sentence fully settled into my entire being. It was the kind of moment where you can never go back and think the same way again. I realized that the people, the places, the partners, and the amount of money I earned had changed in my life. However, my feelings toward myself had remained the same.

At that moment, I knew this had nothing to do with my boss or any other boss I had ever had. This was all about me. I really did not believe I was worth it! I couldn't see my own worthiness. Now, on the surface, to look at me, you would never have been able to know that. I had already achieved beyond what I had dreamed possible for myself. I was living beyond my dreams, and I still didn't believe I was worth it. I conquered cancer, and I made a decision to live without regret. Yet I didn't believe I was worth it.

But that was on the outside. There was a different version of me on the inside. The version that only I knew about.

Can you relate? Others are telling you how worthy, how valuable, you are, but you can't see it?

In that one moment, I knew that the most important thing I could do for myself was to value myself. To know that I was worth it. The reason why I wasn't getting those things I desired was because I was displaying all the signs of not being worthy. You know, the emotions, the resentment, especially of other people in the workplace. I didn't feel worthy so I wasn't asking. Not receiving was supporting my resentment. Resentment further entrenched my lack of worthiness.

I determined that this meeting would witness my ability to ask for what I wanted. More to the point, I would ask for what I had earned and deserved. As I sat in that meeting, my boss presented me with the offer. He added, "I gave you an extremely lucrative cash bonus." *Even though you didn't ask for it.*

I sat there and reviewed the offer then said, "No. That's not good enough." His face dropped because he didn't know what to say.

I imagine he thought, *Who is this woman that just sat in my chair?* I had always just accepted what was offered to me.

I stood my ground. "I deserve and have earned to be paid exactly what I'm worth, and this is exactly what I want." I interrupted my own pattern of questioning my worthiness. Of just accepting whatever was offered to me and being grateful for it. I was confident and ready for the response. He said he would have to think about it.

I left that office, and I'm not going to lie to you. I was thinking, *$#@!!!* It was a swear. *What were you thinking, Tammy?* That was my brain arguing that I had just risked safety. I stood up for myself, and I was suffering from my brain on change, saying, *Are you crazy? What if they fire you? And then you're not going to have a job, and then what are you going to do? Because you're single, and who's going to support you? Oh, no, you don't want to live with your children. That won't be good. Why did you do this? You should've just accepted the offer.*

I bet you have experienced this before when you spoke out in a moment of courage and inspiration and your brain ran wild with negative thoughts, trying to pull you back into what the

brain believed was safe for you. But today, this day, I was having none of that. I kept walking. P.S. I will finish this meeting story in another chapter

## The Dueling Voices

I also realized there were many times I had left money, promotions, sales, or being heard on the table because I was too afraid to ask! I was always waiting for someone to tell me that I was okay, that I was good enough. You're worth getting paid this. You're worth that promotion. You're worth that love. You're worth it.

I had spent almost an entire lifetime hidden behind what I call dueling voices. What's a dueling voice? As women we tend to have the voice we keep inside and the voice that speaks out loud.

The one voice is what I'm saying to you right now, and I'm always asking myself, "What is it that they want to hear?" So that's what I could say. And then the other voice is the voice inside my head where I'm saying what I'm really thinking, but I don't want to say it out loud. Many women, including myself, have lived through or are now in situations of domestic violence. Or as children we lived in households where violence occurred.

That is where my skill of dueling voices is developed, in an effort to avoid conflict, which by the way is impossible; we will only say what we believe the other person wants to hear.

I would like to share this poem I wrote as I recognized later that I had exposed my children to such dysfunction.

### A Child's Voice

My eyes fly open. My ears are alert. These are familiar noises I hear. Mommy and Daddy are having a fight, and this will go on long into the night. My heart beats faster, and the fear starts to grow. I pull up the covers and hide under my pillow. The words that I hear, I've been told not to say. I wonder why they talk to each other that way. The sound of the crash, and things start to break. One piece after another, and my heart starts to ache. Do they really hate each other, or do they hate me? Is this how it is in all families? The voices become quieter as it ends for tonight. When we wake up tomorrow, they will pretend there was no fight. But don't they know, or can't they see, that everything they did was heard and felt by me? A child's voice.

I probably wouldn't have shared this years ago because I would've been embarrassed. My embarrassment would have made me ask questions like, "What's wrong with me? Why did I endure such treatment? Why did I let my children experience this?" But I have overcome that embarrassment. And my choice to be more than my history guarantees that I can sit with any woman in any kind of domestic abuse situation. I can tune in and hear her story. In each case, the common thread is a lack of worthiness.

I can guarantee you this, and this is true for any person in an abusive relationship: it's not you. It is NOT you. I thought it was me for years, but it was not. But what happens is you create these dueling voices. Sounds a little crazy, but the voices are a form of protection. You stop speaking up so nobody hears you. You stop asking for what you want and what you deserve. As women we must remove these dueling voices to live our most passionate life, and the first step is through filling our worthiness tank to overflowing.

*Right: My grandchildren Hunter and Annabelle Below: My son Chad and my daughter Joanne*

## When I Get Confidence

I have led, coached, and mentored thousands of women over the course of my career, and when I ask them what they believe is holding them back, almost all of them say it's a lack of confidence.

When I find my confidence, I will ask for that raise, speak up for what I want, step outside my comfort zone, and live the life I know I deserve.

Are you waiting for the magic moment when fear disappears and confidence appears?

You look outside yourself and notice how everyone else seems to have the confidence that you are patiently waiting for. The confidence to stand up for what you deserve, to do things in life that you want and won't even admit out loud.

Because you don't believe you can have them, you wonder how those other people can be so fearless. What is their secret?

Why can't you be one of the special people who go out and conquer their destiny, filled with confidence and free of fear?

It's time for some straight talking, my love, time to burst this confidence myth bubble that keeps you from living the life you are most passionate about.

Everyone experiences FEAR! As a matter of fact, CONFIDENCE is always DANCING with FEAR.

As FEAR leads, CONFIDENCE follows.

I love dancing on my own and with a partner. In partner dancing, there is always a lead, and the same is true with confidence.

It is a myth that some people, the special people, have developed or were maybe even born with unlimited confidence and a complete lack of fear.

Whenever you step up your game and creep out of your comfort zone to a new adventure, you will feel FEAR.

But guess what? The more you practice confidence, the further outside your comfort zone you are willing to go.

Your dreams live outside your comfort zone.

For today, go out and practice confidence. Sit at the front of the room. Put your hand up first to ask a question.

Introduce yourself to new people, ask someone for help, and even dare to speak out loud one of the dreams you hold for yourself. Practice makes permanent.

You can't "get" confidence, but you can make it easier to dance through the fear to reach your confidence.

I promise you this is true! So, start practicing.

## Speak to Be Heard

We all want to be heard, acknowledged, and understood. In any relationship, business or personal, we want to believe the other person is listening to us, that they understand what we are asking for and acknowledge our concerns. We are not taught how to have conversations that result in being heard and end with us achieving results. We tend to manage these types of interactions with the same level of preparation we give to grabbing coffee with a friend and then sit shell-shocked about why they turned out so badly. There is a different and more strategic method to speaking and being heard. Compelling communication is more than just the words we speak.

## Love Vinegar Agreement

I had a boss who detested conversations about money. We were a startup company, so money was very tight. If I went into his office to ask for something, even if it was fifteen dollars or less, and I started with money, he'd respond with, "Oh no, no, no!" I had to develop my communication and influence skills to push past this resistance and achieve my goals.

I created a version of a method my mom taught me. She would always say, "Use love and vinegar." I have added the final step, agreement.

1. **Love: The first topic should be rapport building—** Start the conversation with praise, stories of success, or something inspirational. It sets the tone for the entire conversation. Even in the most difficult conversation you have to set the tone. This is the most critical skill in communication. Start with love!

2. **Vinegar: The hard topic requires preparation—**This is where you insert any topics, subjects, or comments that you know will be challenging or difficult to discuss. It is your responsibility to be prepared with any data, research, or examples and a proposed solution. I'm not talking about running through the conversation or meeting to the end and determining what the other person will say before they say it. Or before you even have the conversation. You're not a mind reader. I am

talking about being prepared so you are not derailed or taken off-topic.

3. **Agreement: The final topic must be an agreement—** Use the final topic as a time to confirm commitments and agreements so that everyone feels like they've been heard and understands the commitments they have made. The goal is to have everyone leave feeling that it was a win-win, even if you had to have a difficult conversation.

## Dealing with Difficult People

As we close this chapter on how to speak out for what you want, I can't omit one of the most asked questions: "Tammy, how do I deal with difficult people?" Our instinct is to avoid them; however, if you want to move your life forward either personally or professionally, you will always have to interact with people who are difficult. Sometimes it is even the people we love. What follows are my top four secrets and client favorites for dealing with difficult people.

1. **Bring it back to you.** Guess what? We can't control other people's behavior. If we can't change them, what can we do? We can run our interactions with intention. Recognize that when it comes to managing difficult situations or difficult people, all roads lead back to you. It may sound harsh, or even be hard to accept, but the only person you can change is yourself.

2. **Don't take it personally.** Why? Because it's not personal—even though at the time it may seem like it

is. Someone may consistently talk over you, constantly take the conversation off-topic, or appear to be paying less than full attention. When our worthiness tank is low, we can automatically assume that their behavior is intended to annoy or offend us. Instead of letting that thought take over, know your worth and the value you are communicating. Repeat to yourself: *This is not personal. This is not a personal attack.*

3. **Don't get defensive.** Defensiveness is a normal response when someone disagrees with our approach, contradicts our opinion, or questions our suggestions. The experience can immediately "get our back up" and put us on the defensive. Instead, I suggest you view this as an opportunity to uncover something new or to look at something from a different perspective. People who see things differently teach us the most. Make a habit of seeking them out and asking for their opinions. When you notice that rise of defensiveness, repeat to yourself: *This is an opportunity, not a roadblock.*

4. **Don't justify.** When we feel that we are under personal attack, we become very uncomfortable. When we are uncomfortable, we keep on talking to justify what we are saying. We will go into all the reasons why the person should listen to us. This can create an even more challenging situation.

Instead, stop talking. Turn directly to the person, look them in the eye, and say, "I hear what you are saying," "I understand your concern," or "That's a great point."

Follow this with your statement of what will happen next. Perhaps you state that you will discuss this with them later, or maybe you will decide that you don't want to discuss this with them at all.

Remember you can decide how you want to be treated and set the expectations for others to follow. Don't miss out on something you need, want, and deserve by avoiding difficult conversations. Learn to speak out!

*Me in my thirties*

# I LOVE MONEY

**A**re you reading this chapter title and cringing inside? *Why would she say she loves money?* I want to challenge you right away to reprogram your mind concerning money. Money is not a bad word, and neither is selling. I find that it is the most important message I teach to women. Your passion will include money and selling if it is to be lived and sustained. You can love what you do and hate selling. But you cannot sustainably do what you love if you don't make any money at it. You will have more freedom to do what you love when you are successful at selling and are making money.

## Either/Or Syndrome

Okay, remember I said I walked out of that salary negotiation proud but petrified after speaking up and asking for what I was worth? Well, I went back in the next day, and to my surprise I not only received what I was asking for but more! As I said earlier, I was elated; however, I was also overcome with knowing that I had left so much on the table up to this point in my life by not being able to ask. A couple of weeks later I had another one of those life-defining moments. I realized that if I could do this, what else could I do? And I quit my job. My children thought I was crazy. It was so against my character and my belief about security. I was empowered by my own worth and made courageous by learning how to ask. I was going to create my destiny. I must confess at this point I didn't even know what I was going to do as an entrepreneur or what my destiny would end up becoming.

I came across a course that taught you how to speak and sell, and I decided to take it. Then I was invited on a mastermind, to Las Vegas. It was just the leader and about four or five other women. We were there to work on our signature talk and elevator pitch. I thought, *That sounds like a great idea. This should be a lot of fun.* I attended full of hope and excitement for the opportunity to be around other women.

Time came for each of us to share our talk with the group. One after another, the women got up and talked about how they wanted to help people. Each was thoughtful and heartfelt and dedicated to their passion. Then, my turn. I talked about what I knew: money. I had been in business my entire life. I was known as a profit maker. When I delivered my talk, their faces went blank.

Money was not something they talked about, even though they were attending a mastermind on how to speak to sell.

Money was a taboo topic. Comments like, "We don't do this for money; I do this to help people," were the measure of altruism and social responsibility. This, for me, was a money-shaming moment. I questioned whether I was a "good" person because I wanted to make money. In that moment, I decided that this spiritual path was not for me. It would take me over two years to recover from that moment and land back in my destiny. The reason I walked away from a lucrative career and a comfortable lifestyle was for destiny, not poverty. It's a cautionary tale, a reminder to surround yourself with people who bring you up, who support your mission.

Most of us suffer with what I call the Either/Or Syndrome where we believe we can have either one choice or another, but definitely not both at the same time.

It is a common syndrome among women and a major stumbling block for building confidence and filling our worthiness tank.

The symptoms of the Either/Or Syndrome can masquerade and show up in some of the following ways. Do you feel like you are in a constant holding pattern? Always doing what you SHOULD do and not what you WANT to do? Working hard but not achieving the success you deserve? Having to sacrifice your true passion to security?

That is what I experienced at that mastermind.

- Either I can be a good person, or I can make money.
- Either I can follow a spiritual path, or I can go into business.
- Either I can help people, or I can make money.

- Either I can be a mom or have a career.
- Either I can have security or follow my passion.

I guess I can't help people according to this group of women—because I wanted to also have money, because I know money is the fuel for your dreams. Here is the truth: there is no Either/Or. We create that inside ourselves. There is no perfect moment when all the stars will line up. Or all the people you have helped will magically decide to pay you. Life is not a choice between one thing or another. Life is about creating ways for everything to work with you.

P.S. When you are filled with self-worth these kinds of external triggers like I experienced at the mastermind event will not change how you feel about yourself or what action you will take. Now I would just say "thanks for sharing your point of view" and not own it personally.

## The Money Won't Come

Here's the thing, everybody asks me about passion. "How do I find my passion? Where is my passion? How do I get it?"

Another well-known cultural fairy tale: just follow your passion and the money will come. Have you heard this before?

NOT TRUE! I want you to follow your passion, but following your passion does not automatically mean you are going to make money. I have met so many broke women entrepreneurs that it is sad. And they'll say to me, "But, Tammy, you don't understand. I just want to help people. I want to help you and you and you and you." Yet most of these women are NOT helping themselves.

The money won't just magically appear. You must run your passion like a business.

There were many times during this entrepreneurial journey when I said to myself, *Are you insane? You had this cushy job with lots of money, and now you want to go follow your destiny?* But the thing is that you can follow your destiny and keep your job. Yet we convince ourselves in our mind, just like I did, *Either I can work at this company or follow my destiny. Either I can be with these women and not like money, or I can have money and not be spiritual.*

You can start your dream whenever you want. A photographer can go out and take pictures and get them posted. You want to be a speaker? Go find a group and get up there. Because then you are a speaker. What in the heck are you waiting for?

We're always waiting for something. But what if your time runs out? As far as I know, there's like one try at this thing called life. And even if you're reincarnated, it's another try.

## Money Is Not Taboo

I don't care who you are, you require money to fuel your passion to live your life and your dreams. I'm going to let this secret out of the bag. Even if I didn't do anything good with my money, I still have a right to earn it. Because it's my right to earn money. And it's certainly your right to judge me for it and then ask yourself if you observe some conflicts with your beliefs. But it's my right to earn money. And as women we don't stand up and own that right and say, "It's okay." And so we end up undervalued, underpaid, and under wealthy.

We had an aunt and uncle in our family who had money. And my mom used to always say stuff about them like, "Oh, they think they're so hoity-toity." Now, have you ever thought that about people who have money? Or, "Who do they think they are?" Have you heard that money is the root of all evil? Money doesn't grow on trees.

I grew up thinking rich people are bad. So how do you think I would attract money with that belief? It would be difficult. We're getting taught and carrying around beliefs that money is a taboo topic. If we talk about the amount of money we make, then of course we are showing off. However, most people are more than willing to hear about the bad things that are happening in your life. Why? We want to be able to feel better about our own lives by believing that other people have it just as hard or worse than us.

Not one person reading this book created money as the currency in the world today. Researchers believe that money was first brought into the human experience as early as 5000 BC. Lydians were the first to mint coins in 700 BC. I don't care what you call it, love selling, heart selling, whatever it is—it's still selling and it's still money. But it is an exchange of value at its core. You give me something. I give you something. That's what we do. And I do love money. I'm proud to say it, and I want every woman to go out there and say, "I love money!"

You are either laughing right now or horrified at the thought of shouting this statement to the world, because you're wondering what other people would say about you. But what if you did? What if you changed your story about money? Where would you be? How much wealth would you have? How much fuel for your dreams? If you could reach the end of your life having had a huge impact or tremendous wealth, which would you choose? Most people choose having huge impact. To choose tremendous wealth would mean it's all about money, and that is not considered a good quality.

But why can't you have both? You don't have to choose. I'm giving you permission, saying that it's okay to have both. Ban that Either/Or Syndrome. You can have wealth and be a good person at the same time. Go after what you want. Make a way for it to happen. There is no either/or. Let's stand up right now and shout to the world, "I love money!" P.S. Do not follow that statement with "And I am going to do good things with it!" "I love money" is a stand-alone statement. Because you deserve to have the fuel for your dreams.

*Money*

IS THE FUEL
FOR YOUR
DREAMS

— *Tammy Sherger*

@iamworthitproject

# Section III
# THE CHANGE

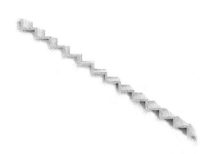

# Chapter 5

# LIVING THE WORTHINESS LIFESTYLE

**M**yth-busting time! Worthiness is a practice, and you must build a lifestyle around it. You don't just find your self-worth one magical day and then keep it for the rest of your life. Saying, great that's done, and now I am worthy. We embrace all different types of lifestyles: fitness, vegan, keto, religion. We put focus and practice into maintaining them every single day. Worthiness is no different. So what is really holding you back from living a worthiness lifestyle?

## The Brain on Change

Your brain does not want change. Our brain is wired to protect us with a fight-or-flight response. This was very useful back in the caveman days when our lives were in constant danger.

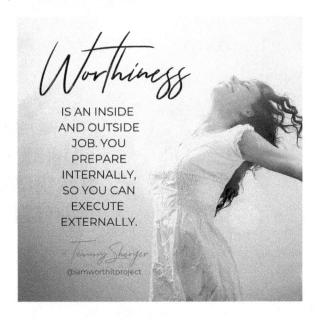

*Worthiness*

IS AN INSIDE
AND OUTSIDE
JOB. YOU
PREPARE
INTERNALLY,
SO YOU CAN
EXECUTE
EXTERNALLY.

— Tammy Sharger
@iamworthitproject

However, this protection mechanism can be triggered even when you are trying to do something new. Even if the something new is good for you. When you get that inspired moment and you introduce something new, you are excited until your brain starts processing the change.

Have you noticed when you have moments of inspired confidence and you make a decision to chase after your dreams…it is usually followed by a roaring waterfall of swirling reasons why you shouldn't follow through on the commitment you just made.

This is your brain on change. It is trying to protect you by keeping you the same. And your brain is powerful, filled with data—some of it outdated. And it will push all that outdated data right to the surface.

Even now, after all the success I have experienced, when I step out of my comfort zone I feel that impact of my brain on change.

I will hear things like, *Who do you think you are? Do you really think you can accomplish that? What experience do you have? Do you even have the right skills?*

When you experience your brain on change and hear all these statements rush through your mind, just STOP.

Ask yourself, Is this true?

And if that doesn't work, I learned a quick tip to silence my inner critic from Les Brown.

When all those thoughts are swirling around in your brain, just tell them to SHUT UP.

That's right, when you shout "Shut up!" out loud, it actually interrupts the pattern and will stop the flow of negative thoughts.

Don't let your brain run your life; you run your brain.

The brain tries to protect you by keeping you in the same routine. It rationalizes that even an unhealthy routine that doesn't kill you or have unending pain is preferable to an uncertain alternative. To keep you the same, it brings to the surface every reason why you should stay in your comfort zone. *I don't have enough money. I don't have enough time. I don't have enough people to support me. It's never going to happen for me. Who do I think I am that I'm going to be able to do that?*

You must remain consistent in the practice of your new routine because the minute you try to change your habits, remember you will experience your brain on change. Instead of believing "I never stick to anything; I just can't do it," recognize that is not it. The difficulty is because your brain is trying to go back to comfort. You change that by recognizing that your brain believes it is trying to protect you. But remember you are in charge of your life and you are in charge of training your brain.

As human beings we are all running a routine every day, and you have a choice. Run a good-for-you routine that leads you to living your best life, or stay stuck in a feel-bad one.

Have you ever tried to play a record that is scratched, and the needle gets stuck? It just goes over and over the same word. Your brain is just like the scratched record, repeating the same thoughts it believes you need to hear to stay safe. You must actively lift the needle over the scratch. That's why we tell the same story over and over again, because our brain is stuck in a loop. I call this a brain loop. You must interrupt this pattern. You must manage your brain through the change.

Here's what it is not. You are not bad. You do not lack willpower. You are not a failure. There's nothing wrong with you. As you sit here right now, there's nothing wrong with you. It is your time to stand up and take charge of the story of your life.

It's not who you are that holds you back. It's who you think you're not. Everything you want to do is right there. It's right there for you. And it's hard to believe that that's true, that that's possible, when you're carrying that old story and all those old beliefs. But that doesn't go away; you make a choice, a decision, to let it go. To do something different. You are never too old or too young to start. Make the decision before your time runs out. I hate to tell you, but for all of us one day that's going to happen.

Be aware of death, not afraid. Decide that you no longer want to live the Robot Lifestyle where you wait for your life to just happen, but instead you take charge and create the life you choose to live.

## The Secret to Change

Yes, change can feel hard! Especially when we rely on the traditional methods of change. When we believe change is easier for some people, that we would change if we had the willpower. But what if you could take advantage of the most powerful tool you already have? What if you could understand how to train your brain? How many of you have ever thought about training your brain? We don't get taught this kind of information. Unless we go out and gain a certification in coaching or a degree in neuropsychology, most of us don't study the brain and how it works.

I have studied the brain and how it works out of a childhood fascination. I've truly spent my entire life learning. I have invested tens of thousands of hours and dollars in my quest to live without regret. Neurolinguistic programming (NLP) is one of my favorite constructs. I was introduced to NLP at a coaching course founded on that construct. Simply put, what NLP teaches you is how your brain drives your behavior. In the Worthiness, Wisdom & Wealth for Women program I share with you my proprietary secret, the secret that has allowed me to achieve extraordinary success not only for myself but for thousands of others.

## The Power of Worthiness

Consistency is the secret to making it a lifestyle, to experiencing years of living your dreams, not just a flash in the frying pan or a one-off success. Worthiness is a practice. You must build your life around it.

We have no problem focusing on the external, but the internal workings, the stuff that drives our behavior, falls into the afterthought category. Until we face a crisis, until we are in turmoil, perhaps then we shine a light on the inside. It's not surprising that worthiness, our value, and more internal topics are all taboo, left to be discussed with a professional, not topics of general conversation. We put on our masks of I-am-okay and everything is wonderful. They are firmly on our face as we head out into the world each day.

The problem? It doesn't work and our attention is constantly focused on what is wrong with us. What if you did something different? What if you put yourself first, became the best and highest version of yourself? Only one missing ingredient is preventing you from living that life beyond what you ever dreamed possible for yourself.

The missing ingredient is your sense of worthiness.

## The Worthiness Practice

Until the moment I was diagnosed with stage two breast cancer, the moment when I asked if I was going to die and the doctor said he didn't know, I believed that life just happened. I was waiting to see what life would deliver to me. In that moment I experienced such an overwhelming feeling of regret for the things I had not done. I didn't know at the time that my promise to myself to never experience that feeling again would take me on a journey of worthiness. The secret hidden behind the regret, the regret for the things I hadn't done, was that I didn't believe I was good enough. The truth behind why I never went after any of the dreams I had? I did not believe I was worth it.

I know I am not alone in this. The lack of worthiness shows up in your life disguised as unhappiness, resentment, a feeling of being overworked and undervalued. It shows up as bad relationships, feeling stuck, low expectations, and living small.

Perhaps you tend to get stuck in the past.

It just seems like the same bad things keep happening, right? Like you can't ever catch a break. And so you think... well, what's the point of trying to change things? Why should I even try when it backfires every time?

Sound familiar?

I understand how you feel. I felt that way too. Then I realized that I could rewrite my own story. I could choose to take control and build the life I truly wanted.

Or maybe you believe like I did that you don't have the right education or skills to be successful. Now, my story alone should prove to you that is just not true.

It doesn't matter what has happened in your past, it doesn't matter how bleak the future may seem or where you are starting from right now. You too can build the life you dream of.

And I know it is hard to take risks, especially when they go against what you've been taught is the right way to do things. Maybe you'll be safer and happier if you just don't make waves, right?

Deep down inside, you know that's not true. Otherwise, you wouldn't be drawn to this dream. You wouldn't feel that longing for something more.

All those hard days at work. All the times you've been overlooked. The times you waited for someone else to realize what you wanted and hand it over on a platter. The times someone else got the promotion...

It's because deep down inside you don't feel that you're worthy. And *I know*, it's hard to discover that the thing holding you back is not external. That it's something YOU can change. But don't blame yourself. It's all down to the beliefs you were hypnotized with as you grew up.

You keep thinking, *Tomorrow. Someday I'll be ready, but it's not today.* I have to tell you, if you keep saying tomorrow then someday will turn into never.

The journey to worthiness and the success it brings takes place day by day. And don't worry, I'm not talking about just positive thinking your way to a new life.

You need to learn how to execute on your dreams every day in a way that allows you to be the very best version of yourself. I'm talking strategic plans that give you the tactics you need to achieve the big goals you have. The next promotion. A raise. Starting your own business. Making the management team. No matter what YOUR dream is, you can make it happen if you understand the REAL secrets to success.

Because when you feel worthy, life doesn't feel like a grind.

When you feel worthy and stand in your confidence, success *isn't* just for other people.

We are taught that there's a right path. That's the path successful people take. But in reality, there is no one way to reach your dreams.

**The thing successful people have in common is a belief in their worth, in the gift they must give to the world.** *And a strategic, tactical plan to reach the life they dream of by* **harnessing the secrets to success.**

You *can* do the things you really want. You just need to discover these success secrets and start working on them today.

I urge you to remember this! Your sense of worthiness is made up of your beliefs. A belief is only a statement that you have decided is true. You can change your mind; you can delete the data that is working against you. You can replace the data with new beliefs, beliefs that you decide are yours, not ones that were implanted into your brain years ago as a child. You can delete the beliefs that you allowed to enter your brain from other people's opinions of you. You, my love, can decide your own value, your own worth!

Join me now as I take you through the secret practices of the Worthiness Warrior. You are not alone. Let me take you by the hand and shine the light on how you too can create the life you dream of, the life you deserve. The world is ready for you to step into that. Come with me on the Journey to Worthiness. Because you—you, my love—are worth it!

# Chapter 6

# EXECUTE IT IN THE REAL WORLD

**T**he success connection—the success trifecta, as I like to call it—is when you elevate your worthiness, wisdom, and wealth.

Feeling good is not enough; traditional education on its own is not enough to create the success that leads you to the life you deserve.

The ability to go out and execute in the real day-to-day world of business and life is what gives you the success advantage.

The beginning of this book showed you how to bust down the barriers created by hidden beliefs, the beliefs that are mostly formed as children when we do not have the ability to decide which beliefs are good for us and which ones we need to delete.

These hidden beliefs drive our daily behavior and show up as unhappiness, worry, and doubt. The never-ending chase to feel good enough.

You can now unleash the power of your brain. Your own personal computer to create new routines and rituals that work for you, not against you.

And now I want to share with you my personal business strategies, namely how to use compelling communication. This type of communication is more than the words we speak. Just as you can create the life you want, you can also create the career or business you want too.

I have been fortunate enough to work with companies that deeply understood the power of communication without words.

I recall the first day of my nineteen years with Costco Wholesale, thinking to myself, *Why would people pay to shop when they could do it for free?* After working my way through all areas of operations, including the successful introduction of a second-tier membership, the Executive Card, I still marvel at Costco's commitment to keep its core promise to its members, their ability to bring value to their members day after day.

And now in my second startup, I continue to marvel at how these key teachings, my favorite strategies, when put into action will set you apart from the competition.

Remember this: knowledge is your kindling for a firestorm of action. Because action is where the transformation takes place.

Get ready to execute in a new way.

## Be Unique in Competitive Markets

Have you ever heard the saying "perception is reality"? Are you creating the perception of your business, or are you just letting it happen? The perception of you as a business, as a professional, is either consciously or subconsciously being built upon small details. The potential client continues to pull from these small details in their decision-making process to answer the question, Do I or do I not want to conduct business with this person or company?

Your goal as a business owner, entrepreneur, or sales professional is to ALWAYS have your potential clients and current clients answer that question with a resounding YES!

It doesn't cost money to be unique and to have that potential client say YES. Throughout this chapter I'm going to break down the things you need to do to keep them saying YES. Up to now this book has been relational—me showing you how to embark on your own worthiness journey (and why). Now it's time to get nitty-gritty in the details of making yourself stand out from the crowd.

### *Use Professional-looking Documents*

You don't need to spend thousands of dollars to create professional documents to send out or bring with you when you meet your potential clients. Use Canva to create documents, checklists, or agendas that you can use over and over again.

PDF Escape has a free option where you can upload your PDF and make it a fillable form so it can be completed online.

Always use spellcheck and have another set of eyes check your documents for errors. A great tip to catch mistakes is to read the information out loud.

Professional documents build instant credibility for you and your business; you are seen as a professional.

### Use an Agenda

An agenda serves as a roadmap, a checklist of what needs to happen in your meetings. It allows you to be fully present and listening because you are not thinking about what has to happen next. The agenda also sets your potential client at ease because clients like to be able to predict what is going to happen. Perhaps best of all, an agenda makes it easy to ask for the sale because you both know not only that it is going to happen but when.

Having an agenda sets you apart from other business owners. The perception created is that you are a professional because you took time to prepare and have a plan. This is a great way to build credibility and trust.

### Always have a Goal

It is unlikely that your client will tell you, but if they feel you are wasting their time, they will not do business with you. Clients want to see and feel progress. Setting and achieving goals provides this feeling of progress for your client and enhances your credibility. It's a simple yet powerful strategy that builds upon our human need to feel a sense of accomplishment, to feel successful. Your clients will experience progress in every interaction with you and your business. A great goal for that first meetings is "I want to demonstrate the value I can add to your business, your life, etc."

In short, by having a goal you will be viewed as a person who "gets stuff done."

### Set the Stage

What type of setting is your client walking into, and what does it say about your business? If you are meeting at a coffee shop, have you checked it out in advance? Is it clean? Will you be able to have a conversation or get a seat? If it is online, will your technology work? What will your potential client see or hear in the background?

Location will tell the story of you as a business. What do you want your potential client to think?

### Build Rapport

Rapport is a skill defined as the ability to relate to others in a way that creates a level of trust and understanding.

Do not start your meeting, your phone call, your email with a negative topic. This will set the tone even if it is done subconsciously. Always start with a positive story or upbeat comment.

Be aware of your body language, tone of voice, and facial expressions especially if you are having a challenging day or just coming from a difficult meeting. Don't let it carry over.

Rapport doesn't just happen; you make it happen with the details.

### It's Not About You

Stop talking. When you find the sales process challenging, you may tend to spend too much time talking about YOU. Why? You are trying to demonstrate your credibility. In an introductory meeting you should have two to three questions to ask your potential client so you can learn more about them. Here are some examples:

- If our business relationship worked out exactly right for you, what would you see as the end result? Be specific (i.e. "I want to have ten more clients").
- How important is it for you to achieve this result right now on a scale of 1 to 5, with 5 being "there is nothing more important for me right now"?
- What prompted you to meet with me today?

Remember, it's not about you. The meeting is about your potential client. Have questions that make them feel heard and acknowledged and you will be able to frame your services as the solution to their problems.

### Bring Value

Always, always bring additional value to your meeting. The same as when you are invited to have dinner at a friend's home, and you bring them a gift. Perhaps it is a checklist or resource that will solve a problem for them.

They feel valued and appreciated. It creates a bond. When we receive a gift from another person, we are more likely to give something back in return.

### Recap

Recap what you have heard so far in the meeting. Use statements such as "I just want to make sure I have captured what you have said." Try using the same key words the potential client has used to describe what their point of pain is and what they want to accomplish.

The person feels heard, acknowledged, and understood. "Wow, this person really gets me."

### Next Steps

This is where you close your sale—depending on how long your sales funnel is (can you close a sale in the first meeting?). Knowing your sales funnel will determine if you are asking for the sale in the first meeting or setting up the next step in your funnel. Here are some examples of closing lines:

"The black one appears to be your favorite. I will write that up for you right now."

"From what you said, I can tell that xxx is the solution for your problem. I will fill out the paperwork."

By the time you get to next steps you have already set the groundwork for a YES.

### Meetings Do Matter

When people think about meetings, they usually picture a boardroom with a bunch of people sitting around the table, but in reality, every time we interact with another person during our workday or in business, we are having a meeting—we just don't call it that!

I would like to start with one of my favorite quotes by Booker T. Washington: "Excellence is to do a common thing in an uncommon way."

Ponder that for a moment, that it's possible for us to discover solutions when we do a common thing in an uncommon way.

Here's the paradox, though. When people talk about finding solutions to common business issues, we all face— employee productivity, employee performance, or employee engagement, for example—we often believe there has to be a massive upheaval, a big new initiative. Or maybe we even hope for that magical program—you know the one—that will drop down from the sky and solve all our business issues for us.

But what if...?

What if you already had the tools you needed, you just didn't know it, and you didn't know how to maximize their impact and influence?

And, in fact, what if the tools and skills to manage and solve those common business issues were right there, just waiting for you?

I would like to tell you a quick human resources story. It happened when I decided to change careers and landed in this role at a startup company as an HR manager.

Keep in mind I had been an operational person my entire career; I was known as an operational strategist.

Honestly, I thought, *How hard can this HR thing be?* I had been successfully leading people my entire career.

It was really hard. I no longer had direct contact with people or the ability to manage their achievement of day-to-day tasks. And not only did these people no longer report to me, but neither did their managers, who were not always fully supportive of the time I asked for to be spent in training and away from the core business.

I admit I had a crisis of confidence in this role because what had usually been so easy for me to accomplish had now become quite difficult. I had all these results I was expected to achieve. I'm sure you are familiar with them: productivity, performance, accountability, and a world-class leadership team. All this through people I had no direct contact with!

So at first I tried suggesting tips to the managers, ones that had worked for me as a leader. I was talking but no one was listening.

And then I thought, *I'm going to bring it up in our managers meeting*, and that didn't fly very well either.

I finally had an aha moment where things became crystal clear.

I realized I had been trying to TELL them what to do, and that wasn't going to work for me. I had to find a way to incorporate the tools and skills I knew—based on my past experience—would lead both the people and the managers to success. I also had to incorporate these new tools and skills into their day-to-day behavior. I had to find a way to slide them in kind of unnoticed…

Now that's how the seeds of Master the Art of the Meeting got planted. They started from my experience as an HR manager.

I continue to build all my businesses around doing a common thing in an uncommon way.

Do you want to be unique in competitive markets, build better professional and personal relationships, and create success that others can't see? Learn how to communicate with influence in your meetings.

Meetings can be used to instill desired corporate behavior—things like being on time, keeping commitments, accountability, and achievement of common business goals. By taking a practice such as the meeting, a repeatable action that people have over and over again every day, and giving it a "system," those very meetings can transform productivity, performance, and results.

- Own the room—You must be able to command your audience's attention from beginning to end.
- Let people know what to expect so you have their full attention.
- Make eye contact with everyone in the room so they feel acknowledged.
- Set the stage—Let people know you are in charge of the outcomes. Start with the end in mind.
- Define the parameters of the event and how anything off-topic will be addressed.
- Stand firm in the direction you are heading.
- Don't let others take you off track.
- Use stories to tell your story.

You don't have to be perfect you have to connect.

If you want to influence, you have to lead the conversation not follow.

Do you want to influence others, hold people accountable, set the standards of behavior? Learn how to run the meeting, the training session, the brainstorm, the conversations. Be the person who not only delivers results but can bring others on board to deliver results as well.

I loved my career at Costco. However, after nineteen years I wondered if there was anything else I could accomplish. Was this all there was, and would I work here until I retired? I made the decision to leave, and when I look back the only dream I had was to have an office with a door.

At this point in my career I had spent many hours in meetings that did not produce results. Then the next week we would do it all over again. Although people complained, we also believed that was just the way it was. Nothing could change.

Three days into my new role at a startup company, I had a meeting with the CEO. I believed I was prepared. I had my list of things to discuss, and I headed into the meeting confident that I was ready.

His first question: "What's your goal for this meeting?" I sat up straight and responded with the items on my list.

"That is not a goal," he replied. "What are you going to leave the meeting achieving?"

I couldn't answer, and he said, "I don't have meetings with anyone unless they have a goal."

The meeting was over, the lesson learned. This was day one of learning that to be influential you have to lead the conversation.

Let me repeat that: if you want to influence you have to lead the conversation, not follow.

Do you want to influence others, hold people accountable, set the standards of behavior?

## Three Stages to Owning the Room

**BEFORE**

1. Prepare Meeting Strategies

   A successful meeting begins with preparation, not the invitation.

2. Select a YES

   Your YES is the foundation on which the entire meeting is built.

3. The Power of the List

   Once you know your goal, you must decide who you need at your meeting to help you achieve it.

4. Set the Stage

   Where and when you have your meeting is the strategy to ensuring your guests are at their most receptive.

5. Prepare the Agenda

   The agenda is the story, the roadmap of how you are going to lead you and your guests to a Meeting Yes.

6. Send the Invitation

   Now that you have completed the preparation, you can send the meeting invitation.

**DURING**

7. Timing/Efficiency

   As the host, you set the tone for the meeting, arrive first and on time to ensure any technology is functioning, and are ready to go.

8. Introductions

   Introductions are made to cover each person's role and responsibility and/or the topic of the meeting.

9. Parking Lot

   Announcing the "parking lot" at the start sets the expectation that anything off-topic will be parked and that there is a method for all meeting guests to be heard.

10. Rapport

    Start with rapport so your guests will feel good and be more receptive to you and your meeting.

11. Topics/Meeting Management

    The agenda topics are strategically placed to give you maximum impact and influence throughout your meeting.

12. The YES Goal

    As the host, you are always aware that the meeting has one purpose and that is to achieve your goal.

13. Agreements

    Recap what has been accomplished and agreed upon so your guests feel heard, acknowledged, and that they made progress. Guests who leave with a positive feeling are more likely to keep their commitments.

**AFTER**

14. Thank You

    Send a same-day "thank you" to any external meeting guests to show that you value and respect their time.

15. Master Commitments

    If you want to be a credible host, you must respond to all parking lot items within forty-eight hours to build trust.

16. Meeting Commitments

    Especially for standing meetings, if commitments are consistently missed you as the meeting host have to take ownership and hold people accountable.

## The Agenda A Brand Builder

Most people think of an agenda as simply a list of what they are going to discuss at the meeting. Agendas are often thrown together without much thought, or even created on the fly in the first few minutes of the meeting ("Hey, anyone have any topics they'd like to add?").

But what if you started thinking of the agenda as a strategic ally?

As professionals, leaders, and business owners we assume that everyone knows and understands the vision, the core values, and the why of the company. They don't. In a world full of distractions and noise, repetition is key in helping important messaging sink in.

The agenda used in every meeting allows you to set the stage for your brand, culture, and values both as an individual and company.

I have been involved in building startup companies. When you are at the stage where you have no money, no projects, no credibility to bring to the table when meeting with potential clients, you can create credibility by how you conduct your meetings.

### The Details: Time, Location, Duration

These components of the Agenda set a high standard of respect and value for people's time. When "start on time, finish on time" is the only acceptable standard for a meeting, people will raise their performance to meet this standard, and this will flow over into all other areas of their workday activities. It also meets the human need for feeling a sense of progress, of moving forward.

### The Meeting WHY

Teach people the difference between big-picture and detail thinking and how it impacts the achievement of goals. The meeting WHY is always big-picture thinking. This is why most meetings fail to get stuff done. People often go into meetings with the WHY they are getting together, not the goal they must achieve. For example, the WHY is "we are discussing the new software we are installing." The goal is "we will assign responsibility of the tasks." Notice the difference and how the WHY could have your meeting going off into many different directions whereas your goal will keep you focused on your end result.

### The YES Goal

You can't get somewhere if you don't know where you are going. You must know your YES goal before you have a meeting. This teaches people how to build a roadmap of small, achievable goals that lead to their big-picture end results. This creates a culture of accomplishment, one meeting at a time, and serves the common human need to be successful.

Below are some success strategies for meetings that most people do not even consider. Review each step and how you can use it to build credibility with clients or build culture in your company. Success is in the details that are practiced again and again—eventually without even thinking about them.

Introductions (2 minutes of meeting time)

How often do you host a meeting and just invite everybody? Thinking about the people you are inviting as your "guests" changes how you treat them at the underground decision-making level. Put the same effort into your meeting guest list as you would to the guest list for a personal event you are hosting.

Cement a Core Value (1 minute of meeting time)

You can't expect a mission statement or your core values posted on the wall in a frame to actually work. They are just words; you must incorporate them into day-to-day operational activities.

Repeating them over and over allows them to become part of your underground decision-making process.

Accomplishments (1 minute of meeting time)

We all need to feel a sense of accomplishment, that moment at the end of the day where we can sit back and say, "Look what

I got done." This daily dose of feeling brilliant is what drives us to keep trying. Small daily recognized achievements lead to the creation of a Culture of Accomplishment.

Housekeeping (1-5 minutes of meeting time)

Having a consistent process for distributing information ensures it is heard and understood by your employees. Make sure all information is broken down into small, easy-to-consume pieces.

Town Halls are housekeeping on a big scale.

Parking Lot

This is meetings gone wild, where everything but the topic of the meeting is discussed and you end up having what I call "Groundhog Meetings"—the same meeting over and over again, never ending in a decision. This leads to all types of negative results: the meeting host and the other guests are frustrated, you lose credibility and employee engagement, and the company loses clients, sales, and opportunities.

And let's not forget about productivity. Always have a Parking Lot this is the place to park off topic items.

Commitments

Getting stuff done—that is what we all want to have happen in our workday. Having clearly defined commitments with due dates and timelines helps get stuff done.

Commitments improve co-worker relationships when we can rely on each other to achieve common goals. They set a standard of accomplishment.

<u>Recap</u> (1 minute of meeting time)

We all want to be heard, understood, and acknowledged. And we want clarity so we don't make mistakes. When we feel this in the workplace it increases our drive and desire to meet individual and company goals. It inspires an engaged environment with everyone working toward the same vision.

### The Power of the Guest List

If you want a YES, invite the right guests. We touched on this earlier, but now let's dig a little deeper. What would happen if you started to view the people you are inviting to your personal or professional meetings—the attendees—as your guests?

Just making a simple shift in the language you use to describe a person can alter the way you treat them.

How much time would you spend on the guest list for a wedding or a special event? Your thinking might go something like this: *Which relatives or friends should we invite? Do they get along with each other, or do we need to sit them at separate tables?*

Yet we believe that we can achieve our goals in business communication without much thought to who needs to be there and what we want them to contribute.

Here are some examples of the different types of guests you may need to achieve your YES.

### Guest Type: Decision Maker

Their role: I have reached a certain level of authority where I can be the final decision maker on certain topics.

**Guest Type: Internal Subject Matter Expert (SME)**

Their role: I am one of your co-workers with a specific skillset. I have the expertise to support the material and/or request you are presenting at the meeting.

**Guest Type: External Subject Matter Expert (SME)**

Their role: I am a person with a specific skillset that is from outside your company. I have the expertise to support the material or requests you are presenting at your meeting.

**Guest Type: Project Cheerleader**

Their role: I am a member of the leadership team, and I support the project you are working on. I have built a high level of trust and credibility, and people respect my opinions.

**Guest Type: Key Leader**

Their role: I am a member of the management team responsible for a specific area or department that would be impacted by decisions or actions that result from your meeting.

## Meetings—a Culture Builder

Earlier I told you that meetings can be used to instill desired corporate behavior and that by giving meetings a "system" they can transform productivity, performance, and results.

And here's the thing: this solution comes with its very own magic sauce. People already hate meetings; they already feel like meetings are dragging them down.

- Running from meeting to meeting with little to show for it
- Constantly chasing people down and trying to hold them accountable
- Getting to the end of the workday only to realize it's not over
- Feeling like you're talking but no one is listening
- Being unable to achieve your business goals even though you are working hard
- Wasting time in meetings that could be better spent doing your real work—the job you were hired for!

So people are very receptive to changing meeting behavior, and it becomes a win-win for both the employees and the company.

Meetings are used as the strategy for the employees to produce predictable results, and along the way the company realizes a significant and measurable return on investment through the reduced number of meetings, creating savings and the productivity gain (the time savings) of employees focused on the core business.

Maybe you have already spent vast dollar amounts on training that has failed to yield results. Usually the training is an attempt to find a way for a group of different people to work together to achieve common business goals.

Here is the question I get asked: Can we improve results and alignment with company values or desired corporate behavior even though we are all different as human beings, as employees?

Yes, it is possible!

Have you heard the saying "We are all more alike than we are different"? This is a key component of our training, and you will hear me repeat parts of it over and over again. To create an environment where you can instill desired behavior, it is essential that you recognize how much we are all the same.

When I work with my consulting clients, I always start with focusing on how we are more the same as human beings. I learned this from my role in human resources when I no longer had direct contact with people as I did when I was in operations. To connect, influence, and create change, let's focus on our similar human needs. The Circle of Habit demonstrates three ways we are alike as human beings.

## The Circle of Habit

We are all like an iceberg; that's right, an iceberg. You see the top but you are not aware of what is happening below the surface. Statistics show that 80-85 percent of what drives human behavior happens below the surface.

Most of us believe our decisions are made after careful rational analysis. However, in a matter of seconds we can make hundreds of judgments about people and things through our own filters, our own view of the world.

Here's the kicker: most of our judgments, our perceptions that drive our behavior, are happening in the underground process. Just like the iceberg, it is all happening underneath. Most of the time we are not even aware of it.

The hidden part of the iceberg is where your judgments, perceptions, and beliefs live.

Companies often believe the performance of their employees is driven by salary and benefits alone. They are important factors; however, the perception or judgment an employee has of the company, co-workers, or leader is being created via the subconscious level.

The first step is to identify the existing perceptions, judgments, or beliefs that employees have.

This is done by simply listening to the buzz in your business. You know what I mean, the conversations that employees are having person-to-person: "The managers don't listen," "We don't have enough time or resources to do our job."

It's easy enough as a leader to say, "That is not true so I'm just going to ignore it." But the truth is if the employees believe it then it becomes true.

When you identify the judgments and perceptions, you can bring them to the surface in town halls or department meetings and address them.

The open conversation is not dangerous, the silence is. In the silence people will create their own version of the story; in conversation you create it.

### Similar Human Needs

<u>Ease</u>

If everything we do is a struggle, let's face it—we will quit. An employee does not want to feel like they are constantly banging their head against the wall, drinking from that proverbial firehose.

Heard

We all want to be heard, acknowledged, and understood. Employees want to work for leaders and a company they believe is listening to them.

Success

We all want to feel successful, to get to the end of our day, sit back, and think, *Look what I got done today.* I call it getting our daily dose of feeling brilliant!

A Harvard study by Teresa Animable proves this theory. In it she asks employees:

What makes a worst day?

What makes a good day?

Let the impact of this sink in….

Ensuring that employees experience a daily sense of accomplishment, a feeling of progress, of moving forward, can change the employee's perception of the people they work for and of the company for the positive.

### *The Brain: Create a New Pathway*

Do you remember the first time you drove a car and how much concentration and effort it took for every small task?

Fast forward to today. I don't like to admit it, but I know it happens to all of us. We are in our car driving along, and suddenly we realize that our mind was somewhere else—yet we have continued to drive, changing lanes and stopping at lights. Has this ever happened to you?

Driving is a behavior we have repeated over and over again, and it can happen without us even being aware of it.

The pathway is well worn!

A scientific term: automaticity

The more you practice the behavior, the stronger and more automatic it becomes, and you don't have to think about it.

Consider this: What if you can create automatic behavior through repetition without even thinking about it?

What if you decided on the behaviors you required in your business to be successful and incorporated them into your environment through a repetitive business practice—not driving but meetings.

You would be creating a new pathway.

When we take a practice such as the meeting and give it a "system," the message of how you conduct your meetings seeps into your day-to-day operations. Not only that, if how you conduct your meetings is aligned with your core values, then you and your people are living them every single day and it becomes the way you do business.

The meetings create the environment to repeat behavior and form new pathways!

Let's say it again: *automaticity.*

Defined, it means that anything you repeat over and over again for a period of time will go from deliberate conscious effort to becoming automatic.

How long does it take? It depends on how engrained the old habits are. However, one hundred days is a good timeframe in which to build a new pathway.

## Meetings as Your Vehicle

Meetings can be your vehicle to introduce new behavior to be practiced and repeated over and over until it becomes a habit and creates that new pathway in your brain. The behaviors take on automaticity, and as you reduce the number of meetings you need because they are more effective and stuff gets done, you are tapping into and touching our common human needs to feel at ease, to be heard, and most importantly to feel successful—that daily dose of *I'm brilliant* that we all strive for.

By doing this, you are making a positive shift in the iceberg, creating new perceptions, judgments, and beliefs.

## Employee Experience

So what is an employee experience?

Employee experience is the PERCEPTION employees have of their interactions with you and your organization.

This is not just about their salary or providing a stellar benefit package. The employee experience is a collection of small details at each step of an employee's journey with your business.

It begins the moment your business drops onto the radar of your potential employee. The recruitment process, onboarding system, training provided, leadership interaction… the perception of you as a business is either consciously or subconsciously built upon these small details. The employee continues to pull from these small details in their decision-making process to answer this one question: Do I or do I not want to work for this company? Consider that this questioning starts as soon as your company drops on their radar and continues as long as they are employed.

When the answer is "I do," the employee is engaged; when it is "I don't," they have become disengaged.

It is important to recognize that compelling communication that can change behavior occurs on many more levels than just the words we speak.

Whether you want to or not, you ARE creating an environment, an experience, for your employees.

It's not just what you pay them or the benefit packages.

Here's what I am asking you: Are you deliberately creating it or just letting it happen.

Earlier we talked about using an agenda as not just a list of things to talk about but as a strategic positioning tool.

Learning how to incorporate an agenda into meetings will have clear no-brainer ROI metrics, result in fewer meetings, achieve goals, and elevate your credibility. This alone will offset training costs and reap rewards for the company. Just by adding this piece of paper in every meeting—and making it *standard* in every meeting—will cause people to stop and think about the meetings before having them.

### Strategy First, Meeting Second

That for me is the byproduct. The true ROI comes by using the agenda to create an environment where people can practice and repeat behavior that leads to a sense of accomplishment.

Engaged employees think outside the box and provide solutions to business issues for themselves!

You may not like McDonald's, but it was built on repeatable practices. Culture is built on repeatable practices, how people perceive you or your business is based on repeatable practices.

And meetings are the simplest place to add the repeatable practices into because we have them all the time. We meeting with co-workers, clients, the plumber, the house builder, our hair stylist, volunteering or interviewing or dating. I think you get the picture we are always meeting. And right now, most people are not doing a very good job at it. This is your opportunity to stand out instead of blending in.

Chapter 7

# THE SUCCESS CONNECTION

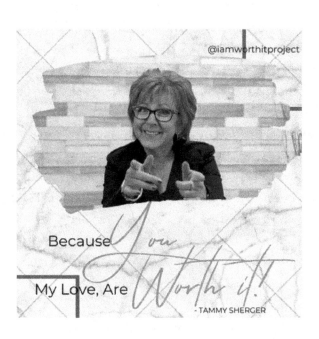

@iamworthitproject

Because *You* ... My Love, Are *Worth it!*

- TAMMY SHERGER

created The Worthiness, Wisdom & Wealth Series to help as many women as possible. Not everyone can afford to work with me one-on-one, and even if they could, I just don't have the hours in the day.

I believe it's vital women start standing up for themselves and discovering how to ask for what they want in a way that leads people to say YES. I lived for too many years not even realizing I didn't feel worthy of the success I dreamed about. I don't want that for you. Don't waste another second of your precious life waiting for your dreams; you have to go out there and get them. We can do it together.

In *The Worthiness, Wisdom & Wealth Series* you'll build your confidence, learn how to sell successfully, gain the tools to stop second-guessing yourself all the time, realize why looking after yourself is an important step in taking care of others (on a plane they tell you to put on your own oxygen mask first for a reason!), and discover how to speak up for what you want without feeling aggressive, selfish, or greedy.

Best of all, you will be able to achieve your goals and dreams without neglecting your family and loved ones *and* build your self-worth to build your net-worth, giving you the freedom to choose how you live.

This is unlike any other training you have taken before. I took the traditional training model and turned it upside down! I want to offer you an experience, an opportunity for me to take you by the hand and walk side by side together down the common human journey called life.

When you finish watching *The Worthiness, Wisdom & Wealth Series* you will:

- Know that YOU are not ALONE
- No longer feel STUCK or LOST
- CHOOSE the life you want to live instead of LETTING life just happen
- Overcome your FEAR of SELLING
- SHOUT to the world "I Love Money"
- Never leave PROMOTIONS, RAISES, and SALES on the table for others to take again
- ASK for what you want, and it will come EASY
- Discover that there is NO CAP on success
- Believe that SUCCESS is not just for OTHER people; it's for you
- Discover that when you feel WORTHY life doesn't feel like a GRIND
- Master the art of COMPELLING communication
- Master the art of INFLUENCE
- Strategically stand out instead of blending in
- Create HUGE IMPACT in your life, the lives of those around you, and the world.
- Elevate your SELF-WORTH and increase your NET-WORTH
- Know the secret practices of the worthiness warrior

After twenty-five-plus successful years in business, working my way up from the stockroom floor to the boardroom table, I have learned a thing or two about what it takes to be successful in business and in life.

I'm not here to tell you what success means to you. I do want to show you that anything is possible. And that the real success connection is when we turn worthiness into wealth.

I have opened up my life to be used in examination. I have shared stories that most of us try to keep secret as we struggle to fit in, to wear our mask of "everything is okay." I share this with you because I know that as each of us as women rises up to our sense of worthiness, we will change this world. Not through external avenues, not through programs, training, and existing methods. But through each individual woman. You, you reading this page right now, know that YOU—you, my love—are WORTH IT!

XOXO

Tammy

*Me in 1963*

*Me in 1965*

"Note to Self ♥
If you FOLLOW
the CROWD
You will end up
in the CROWD"

*Tammy Sherger*

@iamworthitproject

# Chapter 8

# THE UNLIKELY ENTREPRENEUR

**W**hen I share my story of walking away from a lucrative career to follow my destiny, most people say, "I wish I had the courage to do that." The truth is it wasn't courage or confidence, it was that newfound belief in my own worthiness.

I underestimated the challenges that would come with jumping into the life of an entrepreneur.

In hindsight, which of course we all know is so much easier than foresight, I realize there are better ways to make this transition.

However, since most of us suffer from the dreaded Either/Or Syndrome, we believe that we can't do two things at one time. So instead we stick with something we are not happy with, or we make drastic changes because we believe that is the only path to the life we dream about.

My son, a lifelong entrepreneur, laughs when he tells the story of his security-focused mom quitting her job to become an entrepreneur without even knowing what she would do.

I didn't have a specific skillset to take to the marketplace and sell. I wasn't an accountant, lawyer, or project manager.

I was an operational strategist, a person who could see the problem and develop the solution quickly.

What was I going to do with that?

And was that my destiny? The reason I walked away from a lucrative career?

When I left my life as an employee, I thought, *How hard can this be? I will still work, but I won't have to go to an office every day.* Today I can laugh about the craziness of that belief.

The first big change?

My identity. I had worked my way up from the stockroom floor to the boardroom table. Against the odds, I achieved success beyond what I had dreamed for myself as that young girl at Ponderosa Steak House working for $1.35 an hour.

I was now a C-Suite executive, in the upper levels of power in business.

Then I was sitting at a desk in my bedroom wondering what I was going to do now…

You can call it ego, but the truth is when you spend over thirty years going to a job every day, when you invest thirty years into building a career, and then you find yourself sitting at a desk in your bedroom…identity crisis incoming! I can now see how hard the transition to retirement is for people. Most of us spend our entire working career preparing, waiting, desiring the day when we don't have to go to work anymore.

The problem is that by the time that happens for most of us, we have created rituals, routines, and patterns so deep we find that now in this next phase we have no idea who we are or what to do with ourselves.

One of my success secrets was to always hire to my weaknesses. An excellent approach in business. I had an amazing HR manager who could take care of all the things I was not good at.

I quickly recognized that because of that exact situation I had lost one of the other things that had made me so successful: my resourcefulness. I had become accustomed to not having to deal with things that were outside my wheelhouse. The things that would frustrate me, suck up my time, and take me away from the main objectives of my role as a chief administrative officer.

Sitting at my desk in my bedroom, I realized that finding my resourcefulness would be essential to my success as an entrepreneur.

Finally, there is a difference between having a magic money deposit into your bank account every two weeks and having to go out and hunt for your dinner.

As an entrepreneur you have to be able to sell your product, service, or expertise. And the truth is that most people who dump the 9-to-5 don't like to sell. This makes it incredibly difficult to be successful in business. You can love what you do and hate to sell, but you cannot sustain a business that you love if you don't sell.

Now for the good news! When I left my career, it was to follow my destiny. Only I didn't know what that destiny would be. The journey to today as I have pulled that dream, that destiny, into my reality has been like a roller coaster ride.

I have consulted, tested, learned, and kissed a few business frogs along the way.

The decision to build an online business challenged what I believed to be true about myself in the business world: that I was a quick learner, that I could easily solve complex problems, and that since I had helped others successfully build their businesses, building my own shouldn't be that hard.

And then I remember where I started from and laugh at my naivete.

I wasn't even on Facebook, and it took me over three weeks to find someone who could come down to my learning level because I couldn't figure out how to get that square (a post) on my phone.

Now I get teased as I do selfies, post daily, and create content that two years ago seemed impossible to accomplish.

Today as I write this in the I Am Worth It Project Studio preparing to launch a global movement for women, I am amazed at what we as human beings can accomplish.

Because, you see, today I know the one thing that has allowed me to do all the things I used to just dream about:

- build a business doing what I love
- open a studio
- create online courses
- hold live events
- write a book
- and much more…

I believe I am WORTH it and because I did I never QUIT! Even in the darkest of my entrepreneurial days, when I was questioning the sanity of my decision making. When I thought, *I need to go back and get a job!*

I didn't quit! I got up every day and moved the needle forward.

And because I didn't quit, I eventually found the people who could really help me build my business.

Because I believed there is always a way. I found the solutions to the seemingly impossible obstacles.

Because I could place that golden crown of worthiness on my head every day! Even the dark days. I believed it was all possible and that I could make it happen.

The lessons I share now with others wanting to jump into the entrepreneurial life?

First is to be happy where you are. Even if you don't like your job.

Don't dread going to work every day. Appreciate the opportunity to earn income while you plan for the life you truly want.

Your JOB is offering you insight on how to manage and influence relationships, the challenges of business ownership, and many more things.

If you really want to dump the 9-to-5, prepare while you have the JOB because YES you do have the time.

Find a mentor who has already done what you want to do.

That is the quickest path from employee to entrepreneur.

Secondly, success doesn't happen by accident. There is no stamp given to us at birth that determines who will be successful.

But we live with a false belief that success is for special people.

You know the ones I mean.

They are born with a silver spoon in their month.

They have all the luck and of course money.

But that's not true.

There are so many examples of successful people who beat the odds, came from the wrong side of the tracks, started with nothing.

Success does not happen by accident.

You have to do the work.

And where should you start?

With mindset. Because mindset matters.

Whether you believe it's possible or not…

Whether you believe you're worth it or not…

Whether you believe you've got what it takes or not…

IT WILL BE TRUE.

The simplest way to start a mindset transformation?

FEEL GOOD.

No matter what is happening, we always have a choice of how we will react.

When you open your eyes every morning, what is your first thought?

I have trained my brain into a morning ritual so that when I open my eyes, my first thought is, *Thank you! I'm alive, and that means there is hope.*

Because as long as you are breathing you have hope for a good day.

Success will not come to you.

You go and get it.

Finally, as I have chased after bigger and bigger dreams, I have faced an unexpected obstacle: LISTENING TO other people's fears and their false beliefs.

This includes people who are closest to me and even people I have hired to work for me both as individuals and in companies.

When I wanted to write a book, bring one hundred thousand women and now one million women into the I Am Worth It Project Studio, get publicity, and expedite the growth of my business, I have heard…

"Tammy, it's not done that way."

"Look at these experts and how long it has taken them to be successful."

"You can't meet this person, get on that show; it's just not possible."

"The likelihood of that happening is the same as getting struck by lightning."

I could go on.

At first it did impact me. I would hear other people telling me that what I wanted was impossible, and I would question whether I could achieve my dreams and goals.

And then I had an aha moment!

I recognized that I was letting other people—people who had not done what I was doing, who had their own false beliefs—try to tell me if my dreams were possible.

This was their FEAR.

And it was not MINE.

This is why they say it is so important to surround yourself with people who have gone before you and who believe the so-called impossible is actually possible.

If you are surrounded by people who can't at the very least believe it's possible, because belief is free, it's time to expand your circle.

Every day when I open my eyes, I feel so grateful that I made a decision to create the life I want.

I'm grateful that I realized the only thing that came from waiting for what life decided to hand me was disappointment.

It doesn't matter if you are climbing the corporate ladder, jumping into the entrepreneurial life, or somewhere in between.

It doesn't matter if you have achieved success but are asking yourself, *Is there more out there for me?*

The success trifecta for women is found in recognizing their worthiness, the wisdom discovered in connection and mentorship, and growing the wealth to fuel your dreams.

Believe it's possible.

Because belief is free!

# ABOUT THE AUTHOR

Business and life strategist Tammy Sherger is the founder of the **I Am Worth It Project** where she shows women how to harness their self-worth to build a life they're truly passionate about.

As a driver behind one of the most well-known membership models, Tammy learned how to create intrinsic value for members in her nineteen years with Costco Wholesale.

Along with a small team of people, she grew a company from an idea to a $125-million market cap. She realized she was truly capable of success in any type of environment as she grew her career to become a valued chief officer of the company. From the stockroom floor to the boardroom table, she lived beyond what she had dreamed possible for herself as a young girl.

Today, with over twenty years of high-level business experience, Tammy knows what it takes to get that promotion, build that startup, land that raise, and negotiate a "yes" to the things you really want.

Known for her impactful, inspiring, no-fluff coaching, Tammy teaches women—through speaking, live events, her online community, and private one-to-one coaching—how to **stand up**, **speak out,** and **soar** into the life they deserve.

She lives in Canada and teaches all over the world.